THE ECONOMICS OF
POST-COMMUNIST TRANSITION

The Economics of
Post-Communist Transition

OLIVIER BLANCHARD

CLARENDON PRESS · OXFORD

Oxford University Press, Great Clarendon Street, Oxford OX2 6DP
Oxford New York
Athens Auckland Bangkok Bogota Buenos Aires Calcutta
Cape Town Chennai Dar es Salaam Delhi Florence Hong Kong Istanbul
Karachi Kuala Lumpur Madrid Melbourne Mexico City Mumbai
Nairobi Paris São Paolo Singapore Taipei Tokyo Toronto Warsaw
and associated companies in
Berlin Ibadan

Oxford is a registered trade mark of Oxford University Press

Published in the United States by
Oxford University Press Inc., New York

First published 1997
First published in paperback 1998

British Library Cataloguing in Publication Data
Data available

Library of Congress Cataloging in Publication Data
Data available

ISBN 0 19 828926 X (hbk)
ISBN 0 19 829399 2 (pbk)

Printed in Great Britain on acid-free paper by
Bookcraft (Bath) Ltd., Midsomer Norton, Somerset

Preface

Transition in Central and Eastern Europe has led to a U-shaped response of output, that is, a sharp decline in output followed by recovery. Six years after the beginning of transition, most of the countries of Central Europe now seem firmly on the upside. Most of the countries of Eastern Europe are still close to the bottom of the U; an optimistic view is that they are now negotiating the turn.

This U-shaped response of output, its causes and its implications, is the subject of this book. The fact that transition came with an often large initial decrease in output should be seen as a puzzle. After all, the previous economic system was characterized by a myriad distortions. One might have expected that removing most of them would lead to a large increase, not a decrease, in output. This is not what happened. We need to understand why, and to draw the lessons.

The book has four chapters.

The first sets the stage by reviewing the evidence on output, employment, productivity, unemployment, and investment for five Central European countries—the Czech Republic, the Slovak Republic, Poland, Hungary, and Bulgaria. I focus on these countries simply because I know them better. But, while the primary focus of this book is indeed on Central Europe, I shall, as I go along, try to explain differences between Central and Eastern Europe, and—more tentatively, because I know so little—between Central Europe and China.

The second chapter focuses on the basic mechanisms behind the initial decline in output and the later recovery. I argue that there have been two main mechanisms at work. The first is reallocation. Some sectors, such as manufacturing, need to decline; others, such as trade and services, need to expand. I argue that this reallocation process, and its many dimensions, can explain the initial output decline and the initial increase in unemployment. The second mechanism is restructuring. If they are to survive, existing firms need to change their product lines, to close old plants and build new ones, and so on. I show how restructuring can explain both the recovery of output and the continuing high rate of unemployment.

The third chapter examines a number of pieces in more detail. I focus in particular on the adjustment of employment and wages in state firms to the initial shock, on the interactions between restructuring and privatization, and on the relation between reallocation, restructuring, and traffic in the labour market. There are many fascinating and little understood issues here, from the way an insider-controlled firm reacts to a large adverse shock, to how to design privatization so that it leads to restructuring, to why flows in and out of unemployment have been so low despite the high rate of structural transformation. Never has such a political and economic transformation taken place with so much data collected on firms and people as it happened, but we have barely started exploiting the data. My purpose is to sharpen the discussion, and present what we have learned so far.

The fourth, final, chapter is an attempt to put the pieces together. There, I develop an analytical model of transition which incorporates what I see as the central elements of transition: the reallocation from old to new activities, the restructuring of firms, and the interactions with unemployment. I then use this framework to discuss a number of policy issues, from the role of labour market policies, to the design of privatization, to the role of fiscal policy, and to the dynamics of support for reform.

This book is based on three Clarendon Lectures presented in Oxford in late 1995. It builds on research carried out since the early 1990s, and I have many intellectual debts to acknowledge. Andrew Berg, Richard Layard, Marek Dabrowski and Stanislaw Gomulka were companions in my early attempts to understand transition in Poland. Much of my knowledge of firms and labour markets comes from two research projects carried out with Simon Commander and Fabrizio Coricelli at the World Bank. During the course of these projects, I have learned a great deal from them as well as from Tito Boeri, Saul Estrin, Janosz Köllô, Mark Schaffer, and Jan Svejnar among others. Much of my thinking about privatization and restructuring, and about the general equilibrium model of transition presented in Chapter 4, comes from joint work, mostly with Philippe Aghion, but also with Wendy Carlin and Robin Burgess. Michael Kremer has helped me think about the role of disorganization in transition. Whenever I have crossed paths with Jeff Sachs, I have learned a lot. I thank Andrew Boral, Maciej Dudek, Svetlana Danilkina, Susan Ellis, John Keeling, Kornelia Krajnyak, Eric Lindblatt, Piotr Mazurevski, Mariella Nenova, Krzysztof Rybinski, and Andrei Sarychev for their help and research assistance. I also thank Daron Acemoglu, Tito Boeri, Michael Bruno, Fabrizio Coricelli, Ricardo Caballero, Vivek Dehejia, Peter Diamond, Roman Frydman, Simon Johnson, János Kornai, Gilles Saint-Paul, Mark Schaffer, Jan Svejnar and Jerome Vignon for discussions and comments on an earlier draft. I finally thank Andrei Shleifer for many discussions over the years on all aspects of transition.

O.B.

Cambridge, MA
January 1997

Contents

Figures

Tables

1

The Basic Facts

1.1 The Evolution of Aggregate Output

Figure 1.1 gives the evolution of measured GDP in five Central European countries—the Czech Republic, the Slovak Republic, Poland, Hungary, and Bulgaria (C, S, P, H, and B in the figures)—since the beginning of transition. It clearly shows the U-shaped response of output, the initial decline in output followed by recovery. (Data sources for this and the following figures are given in the appendix to this chapter.)

Before taking a closer look, I must justify both the choice of countries and the measurement of time in Figure 1.1.

The reason why I have chosen to concentrate on Central Europe is a simple one: I have a much better knowledge of what has happened there than of what has happened further to the East. One of the challenges facing those working on transition, however, is whether they can convincingly explain the differences between Central Europe, Eastern Europe, and China. I shall try to take up this challenge as I go along. But I shall start from the analysis of what has happened in Central Europe.[1]

To facilitate comparison across countries, I measure time not as calendar time but as time since the beginning of transition in each country. For each country, there is one year in the early 1990s in which there was a sharp decrease in industrial production. I believe that this decrease in industrial production is a good proxy for the change in economic

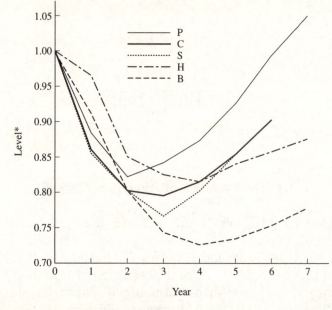

Fig. 1.1. The evolution of GDP
* Value in the year before transition = 1.0

regime, and I take that year to be the first year of transition. This gives 1990 for Poland, Hungary, and Bulgaria; 1991 for the Czech and Slovak republics.[2] I include EBRD forecasts of output for 1996 when available, so that Figure 1.1 gives the behaviour of output for six or seven years of transition, depending on the country. GDP is normalized to be equal to 1 in year 0, the year before transition.

With these preliminaries out of the way, we can return to the behaviour of GDP as shown in Figure 1.1. The figure shows a decline of output for between two years (Poland) and four years (Bulgaria), and a recovery since. All countries are now growing. Based on current estimates, Polish GDP, which declined to about 80 per cent of its pre-transition level, will exceed its pre-transition level in 1996. Bulgaria's GDP, which declined to 72 per cent of its pre-transition level, is lagging behind and is expected to reach only 77 per cent of its pre-transition level in 1996. (For comparison, US GNP stood in 1933 at 70 per cent of its 1929 level. It was back to its pre-Depression level by 1937.)

What Figure 1.1 reports are official measures of GDP. There are many reasons to question their accuracy, especially for the early years of transition. In most cases, base prices used to construct real GDP for those years were pre-transition prices. Activities in the small firms which characterize much of the new private sector were, and still are, only imperfectly measured. And so on. A number of recent studies have looked at the evolution of electricity consumption as a proxy for economic activity.[3] For most of the countries of Eastern Europe, electricity consumption numbers suggest a smaller decline in output than official GDP estimates. But for Central Europe, the numbers for electricity consumption growth are roughly similar to those for GDP growth. For example, in Poland from 1989 to 1994 measured GDP growth was equal to –8.7 per cent, electricity consumption growth to –10.1 per cent. For Bulgaria, the two numbers are –23.7 and –26.4 per cent respectively. The conclusion I draw from these and other studies is that the existence of a substantial output decline is not in doubt, although official statistics probably overestimate its quantitative importance.[4]

1.2 Composition Effects and the Evolution of Manufacturing Output

While activity declined initially in nearly all sectors at the beginning of transition, the decline was far from uniform. Figure 1.2 shows the behaviour of manufacturing output—or more accurately, of the index of industrial production. (The level of production is normalized to 1 in the year pre-transition. The last available year is 1995, and Figure 1.2 therefore covers one less year than Figure 1.1.) The picture is

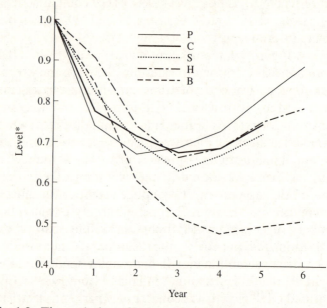

Fig. 1.2. The evolution of industrial production
* Value in the year before transition = 1.0

one of a much larger decline for industrial production than for aggregate output, followed by a weaker recovery. In Poland, Hungary, and the Czech and Slovak republics, manufacturing output declined to somewhere around 65 per cent of its pre-transition level, and the recovery has been weaker than for aggregate output. Bulgaria has had a distinctly larger drop, with production dropping by more than half, and a limited recovery so far.

This worse performance of manufacturing points to an essential aspect of transition, namely reallocation. By the standards of market economies, centrally planned economies had too large a manufacturing sector, too small a service sector. Thus, part of the adjustment must take the form of a reallocation of activities from manufacturing to services.

Can one find, disaggregating further, the pattern of relative output declines one would have expected based on the pattern of initial distortions under central planning? Have the sectors which were protected or subsidized the most suffered the largest drop in output? There is not yet a clear answer to this question. One of the surprising facts of the first couple of years of transition was the lack of such a pattern: most sectors were moving largely together and even those sectors which had been repressed under central planning were typically declining as well.[5] But, over time, there has been increasing differentiation across sectors, and there now appears to be slow convergence of sectoral composition to that observed in OECD countries.[6]

One can get some sense of the degree of sectoral reallocation by constructing the standard deviation of annual rates of change of employment across sectors for each year and each country, a measure first introduced by Lilien [1982] in the context of US fluctuations and now called the 'Lilien measure'. The average value of the Lilien measure (decomposing the economy into ten sectors—agriculture, mining, manufacturing, electricity, gas and water, construction, trade, transport and communications, finance and real estate, and services) since the beginning of transition has been 20.9 per cent for the Czech Republic, 14.2 per cent for the Slovak Republic, 20.3 per cent for Poland, 9.0 per cent for Hungary, and 11.0 per cent for Bulgaria.[7] By way of comparison, the average value of the Lilien measure for the OECD for the period 1990–3 was only 3.4 per cent. This makes it clear that, using Kornai's [1994] expression, the output decline in Central Europe should not be thought of as a conventional recession, but rather as a 'transformational recession'.

1.3 The Evolution of Productivity and Employment

Figures 1.3 and 1.4 give the evolution of aggregate and manufacturing labour productivity respectively. Two facts clearly emerge, an initial decline in productivity, followed by

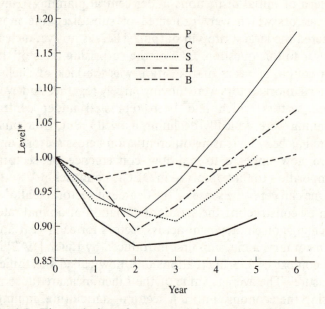

Fig. 1.3. The evolution of aggregate labour productivity
* Value in the year before transition = 1.0

an often large increase since then. The decline has been longer and larger for manufacturing productivity, but manufacturing productivity is also now increasing fast.

Neither the initial decline nor the increase since should come as a surprise. Everywhere in the world, following a sharp drop in sales, employment typically lags behind, and it would have been surprising if state firms in transition economies had behaved very differently. At the same time, there was substantial labour hoarding in those firms even pre-transition, and thus scope for substantial improvements in productivity.[8] These have started to appear.

There are also interesting variations across countries. Perhaps not surprisingly given the size of the output decline, Bulgaria has had the worst productivity performance in manufacturing. More surprising is the poor productivity performance of the Czech Republic, the country which is

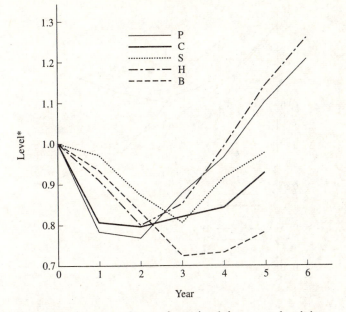

Fig. 1.4. The evolution of manufacturing labour productivity
* Value in the year before transition = 1.0

often perceived as having made more progress than the others, the first country to achieve privatization, the first country to join the OECD.[9]

The implications of the joint evolutions of output and productivity for employment are shown in Figures 1.5 and 1.6, for aggregate and manufacturing employment respectively. As a matter of arithmetic, the fact that productivity has recovered substantially more than output has a simple implication: the evolution of employment looks substantially worse than that of output. (Given the evolution of output, the behaviour of productivity and the behaviour of employment are obviously the two sides of the same coin.) The decline in aggregate employment has been substantially longer and larger than that of output. The decline has ranged from 10 per cent (in the Czech Republic) to 25 per cent (in Bulgaria) of its pre-transition level. Only in 1995

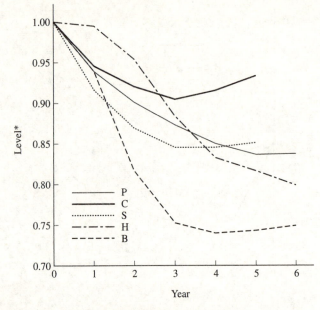

Fig. 1.5. The evolution of aggregate employment
* Value in the year before transition = 1.0

does employment appear to have stabilized. The decline has been larger in manufacturing, ranging from 20 per cent (in the Czech Republic) to 35 per cent (in Hungary and Bulgaria) of the pre-transition level. And there is little sign yet of a turnaround.

1.4 Unemployment

There exist two separate measures of unemployment. One, registered unemployment, is not a very good measure: incentives for the unemployed to register vary over time and across countries. But it is the only measure we have going back to the beginning of transition. The evolution of registered unemployment rates is shown in Figure 1.7. The other

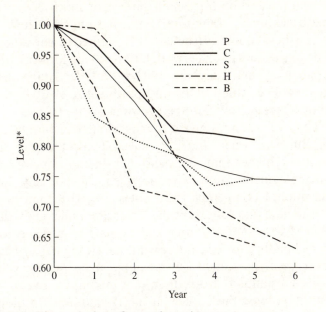

Fig. 1.6. The evolution of manufacturing employment
* Value in the year before transition = 1.0

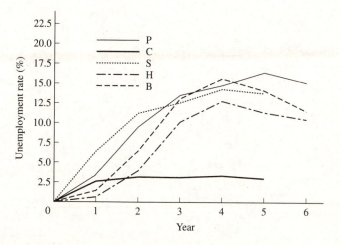

Fig. 1.7. The evolution of registered unemployment

measure, based on household surveys, is much better: the questions are the same over time, and approximately the same across countries (somebody is counted as unemployed if he or she does not have work but is looking for work). But these surveys exist only since 1992 or 1993, depending on the country. The evolution of unemployment rates using these labour force surveys (LFS) is shown in Figure 1.8.

The two measures give a roughly similar picture (except for Bulgaria, where the LFS unemployment rate is substantially higher than the registered unemployment rate). Unemployment rates have increased substantially since transition. LFS unemployment rates are higher than 10 per cent in all countries except the Czech Republic. Only since 1995 have the rates stabilized and, in some countries, started to decline. Just as for employment, the strong performance of productivity leads to an unemployment picture which looks substantially worse than that of output. Even large output growth rates, such as in Poland or the Slovak Republic, have so far been associated with only limited declines in the unemployment rate.

Had there been no increase in working-age population

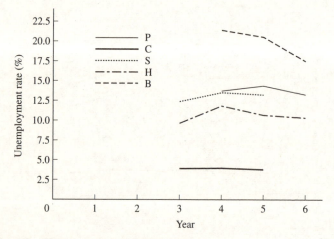

Fig. 1.8. The evolution of LFS unemployment

and no change in participation rates, unemployment rates would range from roughly 7 per cent in the Czech Republic to about 25 per cent in Hungary and Bulgaria. But, as is typical when employment declines sharply, much of the decrease in employment has translated into a decrease in participation. Some workers have retired early, others have given up looking for work, others have shifted to grey- or black-market activities. There are again interesting differences across countries here. To see them, consider the following computation. Let P be the population of working age, N be employment, U be unemployment, and O be non-participation. Then:

$$\Delta P = \Delta N + \Delta U + \Delta O,$$

where Δ denotes the difference between the value of the variable in 1994 and its value in the year pre-transition (1989 or 1990, depending on the country). Consider the ratio $x \equiv \Delta U/(\Delta P - \Delta N)$. A value of 1 for x indicates that the entire adjustment has shown up in unemployment rather than participation. A value of 0 indicates that the entire adjustment has shown up in participation rather than unemployment. The value of x is 0.27 for the Czech Republic, 0.66 for the Slovak Republic, 0.85 for Poland, 0.41 for Hungary, and 0.75 for Bulgaria. Thus, an important part of the reason why the Czech unemployment rate is so much lower than those of the other countries is that much more of the adjustment has taken the form of a reduction in participation (another reason, as we saw earlier, is that productivity growth has been lower, leading to less of a decrease in employment in the first place).

The high unemployment rates in Figures 1.7 and 1.8 convey only imperfectly the nature of unemployment. What matters to the unemployed is not so much the unemployment rate but the probability that they can find a job if unemployed. Indeed, a high unemployment rate is consistent with two very different labour markets: a highly active labour market in which many workers go through unemployment

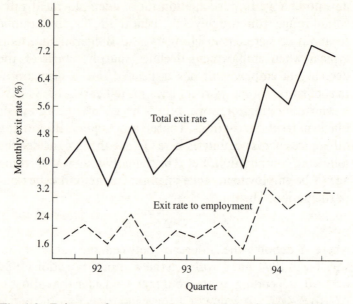

Fig. 1.9. Exit rates from unemployment, Poland, 1992–1995

on their way to other, better, jobs, or a sclerotic labour market in which unemployment is a stagnant pool, and where the unemployed have little hope of finding a job quickly. The US market is very much of the first type. One might have expected the same to be true in the rapidly transforming transition economies. But unemployment in Central Europe is so far of the second type.

This is shown in Figure 1.9, which gives monthly exit rates from unemployment, for Poland, from 1992 to the first quarter of 1995. Figure 1.9 gives two exit rates.[10] The first, given by the solid line, is the overall exit rate from unemployment, defined as the number of people leaving unemployment in a given month as a percentage of the initial stock of unemployed (the figure reports the average for each quarter of the three monthly rates). Many of these people leave unemployment, however, not because they get a job but because they give up on the search. Thus, the second exit rate, represented by the dotted line, gives the exit rate from unemployment to employment, defined as the number of people who leave unemployment for employment in a given month as a percentage of the initial stock of unemployed.

The overall exit rate has increased from around 4 per cent a month to 7 per cent in 1995, at the end of the period. These are very low numbers: compare them to an average exit rate of 36 per cent in the United States. And the picture is worse for the exit rate to employment. While it has increased from 2 per cent a month in 1992 to 3 per cent a month in 1995, this is still extremely low compared for example to an average exit rate to employment in the United States of 24 per cent. High unemployment in Central Europe is not a reflection of high churning. The right image is of a pool of workers with poor prospects of getting jobs any time soon.

1.5 Investment

Given the scope for restructuring, the need for new capital, the relatively low labour costs by international standards, and the high level of human capital, one might have expected transition to be associated with high rates of capital accumulation. For the most part, this has not been the case. Figure 1.10, which gives percentage ratios of gross fixed investment to GDP since the beginning of transition, suggests that the countries fall into two groups. In Hungary, Poland, and Bulgaria, investment ratios have fallen substantially since the beginning of transition; they now range between 20 per cent for Hungary and 15 per cent for Bulgaria. Given that capital–output ratios and thus investment ratios were, however, artificially high pre-transition, this decline must be interpreted with caution.[11] A better way is to compare these investment ratios to ratios in other market economies at roughly the same stage of development. The average investment ratio for Portugal in the 1990s has been 26 per

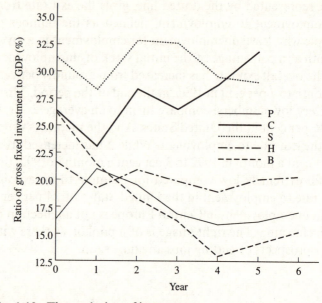

Fig. 1.10. The evolution of investment

cent, that for Chile has been 24 per cent, that for Korea 36 per cent. Thus, investment ratios in these three countries appear quite low indeed. The picture is quite different for the Czech and Slovak republics, where investment ratios are close to 30 per cent. The numbers for the two countries are hard to reconcile with other aspects of the transition, such as the relatively poor performance of productivity. But, despite my efforts, I have not found an obvious problem with the construction of the numbers.[12]

1.6 Perceptions of Pain and Progress

To fully set the stage, let me end by looking at the evolution of perceptions of transition by those who are living through it. Since the beginning of transition in Poland, the 'Centre for research on public opinion' (Centrum Badania Opinii

Spolecznej) in Warsaw has conducted regular surveys of public opinion. It has asked in particular the following two questions:

- What do you think of the current economic situation in Poland? (Bad, Good, Neither good nor bad, Do not know.)
- How do you expect the economic situation to evolve over the next one or two years? (Improve, Worsen, No change, Do not know.)[13]

The two questions refer to the assessment people have of the overall situation, and not of their own situation. But, occasionally, people have been asked the same two questions about their own economic situation; there is a high correlation across different age and socioeconomic groups between the answers to both sets of questions. Thus, it is reasonable to interpret the results as reflecting estimates of their own economic situation, current and prospective.

The basic results from these surveys are plotted in Figure 1.11. The solid line gives the balance of opinion about the 'current economic situation' (proportion of people who think it is good minus the proportion of people who think it is bad) quarterly since the beginning of 1990. The gaps reflect missing data for some quarters. The dotted line gives the balance of opinion about 'expected change' (proportion of people who believe the economy will improve minus proportion of people who believe it will worsen).

What the figure suggests is a very optimistic prior at the beginning of the transition.[14] In 1990, most people found the current situation to be bad; the balance was −68 per cent in the first quarter of 1990. But there was also a wide belief that the economy would soon improve. It did not, at least for a few years. As time passed, and the cost remained high, expectations of change were revised downwards. By the end of 1991, perceptions of the current situation were highly negative, and expectations were now of further deterioration in the future. By 1992 and 1993, things turned around, and

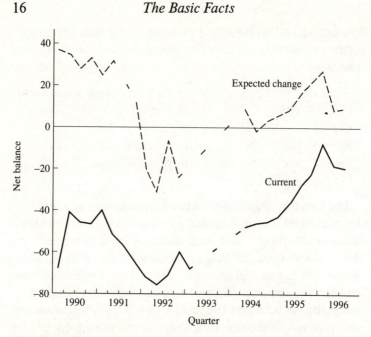

Fig. 1.11. Perceptions of the current situation and expected change, Poland, 1990(1)–1996(3)

both perceptions of the current situation and of the direction of change became more optimistic. While growth started in 1992, only since 1994 have expectations of change become positive again.

This relation between growth, unemployment, and perceptions can be captured through two regressions. Let C denote the balance of opinion about the current situation, E denote the balance of opinion about expected change, y denote the level of industrial production, and u the unemployment rate. Then, the following regressions fit the data well:

$$C = 0.40C(-1) + 0.97y - 1.19u \qquad \bar{R}^2 = 0.82$$
$$(2.7) \qquad\quad (4.8) \qquad (-3.0)$$

$$E = 0.85C + 0.06y - 3.09u \qquad \bar{R}^2 = 0.70$$
$$(2.5) \qquad (0.1) \qquad (-4.7)$$

With the obvious caveat about the limited degrees of freedom (because of missing data, only 13 in each regression), the regressions show how perceptions have moved with both the unemployment rate and the level of industrial production.[15] Unemployment is particularly significant in both regressions. The initial decrease in industrial production and increase in the unemployment rate were associated with both a decline in current perceptions and increasing pessimism about the future. While industrial production has now partially recovered, unemployment remains high. Thus, even in 1995, the fourth year of sustained growth in Poland, perceptions of the current situation were still negative, and optimism about the future guarded at best. Given the democratic nature of transition in Central Europe, these perceptions have played an important role in determining both policy and the behaviour of firms (which have been largely controlled by insiders). This is a theme to which I shall often return in this book.

1.7 Summary and Comparisons: East Germany, Russia

The figures we have seen give a fairly clear picture of the general shape of transition. Transition has led to a U-shaped response of output, a decline of output followed by recovery. Productivity has improved more than output, leading to a sharp decline in employment. Despite an often large decrease in participation, the decline in employment has led to an increase in unemployment, which is only now starting to subside. With the exception of the Czech and Slovak republics, investment rates have been relatively low.

There are also clear differences between countries. Some of them may have more to do with deficiencies of the data than with true differences (the high investment rates, and the relatively poor productivity performances of the Czech and Slovak republics for example). Some appear genuine.

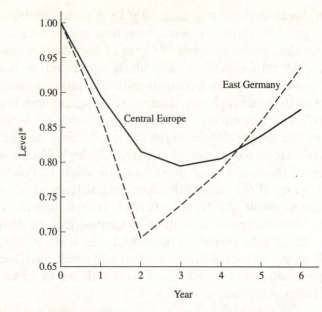

Fig. 1.12. GDP, East Germany versus Central Europe

* Value in the year before transition = 1.0

Bulgaria in particular appears to have had a significantly worse performance. Output has declined more, and recovered more slowly. Unemployment is higher. And the ratio of investment to GDP is low.

My goal in the next chapters will be to examine the mechanisms which can explain these evolutions. Before I do so, let me end this chapter by comparing the performance of Central Europe with the performance of two other countries. The first one is the former East Germany, now Eastern Germany. The other is Russia.

Figure 1.12 shows the evolution of GDP in both Central Europe and Eastern Germany since the beginning of transition. The index for Central Europe's GDP is just the average of the indices shown in Figure 1.1 (with equal weights for all five countries). The first year of transition for Eastern Germany is taken to be 1990. The figure shows how much sharper both the decline and the recovery have been in Germany than in Central Europe. Given the two main specific characteristics of transition in Germany, namely the much larger increase in wages at the beginning of transition, and the much larger capital inflows from Western Germany since, both the sharper decline and the stronger recovery are indeed what one might have expected.

Figures 1.13 and 1.14 show the relative evolutions of GDP and unemployment in Central Europe and Russia.

Figure 1.13 shows how much worse the official decline in output has been in Russia than in Central Europe. The index for GDP in Central Europe is the same as in Figure 1.12. I take the first year of transition in Russia to be 1990, so that the index for Russia's GDP is set equal to 1 for 1989. Six years into transition, measured GDP in Russia stands at under 60 per cent of its pre-transition level, and has yet to turn around. Problems of measurement are much more serious in Russia than in Central Europe, but nobody doubts that there has indeed been a large decline in output in Russia (electricity consumption, for example, decreased by 21.1 per cent between 1989 and 1994).

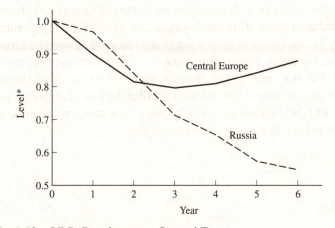

Fig. 1.13. GDP, Russia versus Central Europe

* Value in the year before transition = 1.0

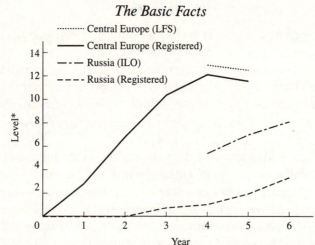

Fig. 1.14. Unemployment rate, Russia versus Central Europe
* Year before transition = 1.0

Figure 1.14 shows, however, that the worse output performance has not been reflected in higher unemployment. The numbers for Central Europe are simple weighted averages of country-specific unemployment rates, registered or LFS. The number for Russia corresponding to the LFS number for Central Europe is not derived from a labour force survey (which is not yet available) but tries to capture a similar notion of unemployment. Registered unemployment in Russia stood at only 3.5 per cent in 1995. Even the larger and the more appropriate measure of unemployment stood at 8.3 per cent. Thus, Russia shows both a much larger decline in output and a much smaller decline in employment than Central Europe. Clearly one of the tasks in the coming chapters will be to try to explain why.

APPENDIX

There are three main sources of economic data in English about Central and Eastern Europe. The first is *Short-Term Economic Indicators: Transition Economies* (STEI for short below), published quarterly by the OECD. The second is *Employment Observatory: Central and Eastern Europe: Employment Trends and Developments* (EO for short below), published by the European Commission. The third is the statistical tables in *The Economics of Transition* (ET for short below), published twice a year by the European Bank for Reconstruction and Development, and complemented by the tables in the *Annual Transition Report*. For those countries which have joined the OECD (the Czech Republic, Hungary, and Poland at this point) or the IMF, data can be found in the OECD *Economic Outlook* and in the IMF *International Financial Statistics*. Data sources and details of the construction of the national income accounts for each country are given in a series of OECD publications.

Data for Figure 1.1 come from ET (vol. 4(1), 1996). Data for the Czech Republic since 1994 come from the OECD *Economic Outlook* (June 1996). Data for Figure 1.2 come from ET. Data for Poland for 1989 and 1990 come from GUS, the Polish Central Statistical Office.

Data for employment used in Figure 1.5 and to construct the productivity numbers in Figure 1.3 come from ET. Data for the Czech Republic since 1994 come from the OECD *Economic Outlook*. Data for the Slovak Republic come from EO (vol. 8, Nov. 1995). Data for Hungary are from ET, except for a correction to the growth rate from 1991 to 1992 (and the subsequent implied adjustment to the level from 1992 on). I use the rate of growth based on data constructed in the same way for 1991 and 1992 as in Blanchard *et al.* [1995, table 7-1]. Data for employment used in Figure 1.6 and to construct the productivity numbers in Figure 1.4 come from EO, with a similar adjustment for Hungary from 1992 on.

Data for Figures 1.7 and 1.8 are from EO. The numbers for 1995 are for the first two quarters only. Data for Figure 1.9 are from personal communication.

Data for Figure 1.10 are from the National Income Accounts,

as published in STEI (1996, third quarter). Data for the Czech Republic come from the OECD *Economic Outlook*.

Data for Figure 1.11 are from various publications of the Centrum Badania Opinii Spolecznej in Warsaw.

Data for Figure 1.12 for East Germany are from the OECD, personal communication. Data for Figures 1.13 and 1.14 are from ET.

NOTES

1. I would have liked to include both Romania and Albania, Romania because of the lack of clear commitment of its government to reform, Albania because of its very sharp drop in output at the beginning of transition. But I know too little about Romania, and the data for Albania are so bad as to be nearly unusable. Thus, I have not included them in this chapter.

2. Using the year in which the country signed an IMF agreement would yield 1990 for Poland and 1991 for the others (see Bruno 1994). Put another way, there was a large decline in production in Hungary and Bulgaria in 1990, i.e. pre-stabilization.

3. Elsewhere in the world, the elasticity of electricity consumption to output has been observed to be close to 1. To the extent, however, that new, service, firms are less electricity-intensive than existing firms, and that the relative price of electricity has increased often substantially, the decline in output in Central and Eastern Europe may well have been smaller than the decline in electricity consumption.

4. For more discussion, EBRD [1995, Annex 11-1]; Kaufmann and Kaliberda [1995]. See also the early study by Berg [1993] on the evolution of consumption and GDP in Poland in 1990. Berg concluded that the decline in output was probably in the range of 5–8 per cent, thus substantially smaller than the official estimate of 12 per cent.

5. See for example the analysis of the first three years of transition in Poland in Berg and Blanchard [1994], or the 1993 OECD *Economic Survey* for Hungary, ch. 4.

6. Commander and Dhar [1996] for Poland and Duflo [1996] for Russia find a significant relation across sectors between the

output decline and 'domestic resource costs', the ratio of domestic prices to world prices pre-transition.

7. These numbers are from Boeri [1996, table 1].

8. For a description of the nature of state firms and the organization of production in Poland pre-transition, see, for example, Sachs [1993].

9. Before making too much of differences in employment or productivity across countries, however, one must understand the limitations of the employment data. Two examples will make the point. The standard series for employment in Hungary show a very large decline in employment from 1991 to 1992, which leads in turn to a large increase in measured productivity in the same year. Much of the decline in employment is, however, the result of a shift in the construction of the series from industry-based to household-based sources. (In constructing Figures 1.3 to 1.6, I have adjusted the series used here to avoid this problem as much as possible. See Appendix.) Or take the surprisingly good performance of Bulgaria's measured aggregate productivity despite the poor performance of productivity in manufacturing. One partial explanation is that, until recently, many people working in agriculture in Bulgaria could register as unemployed, leading to a measured decline in employment in agriculture, and thus an apparent increase in productivity.

10. These rates, which are based on quarterly labour force surveys, do not exist pre-1992. I present Polish numbers only because I do not have corresponding numbers for other countries.

11. For further discussion of capital accumulation pre-transition, look at ch. 1 of the 1996 World Bank report, and references therein.

12. Part of the difference—but only part—is accounted for by the different levels of government investment. Based on IMF estimates, public investment was equal to 7.1 per cent of GDP in the Czech Republic in 1994, compared to only 3.1 per cent in Poland and 1.5 per cent in Bulgaria. This still implies a difference in non-government investment ratios between the Czech Republic and Poland, for example, of more than 10 per cent of GDP. A discussion of the Czech investment numbers, but with no resolution, is given in Jilek [1995].

13. Unfortunately, the phrasing of the question has not been consistent. The question is sometimes about change in the next year, sometimes about change in the next two years.

14. This is the period that Leszek Balcerowicz—who was in charge of economic policy at the time—has called the period of 'extraordinary politics', a period when reforms could be passed which could not be passed later.

15. Somewhat surprisingly (given what we know about perceptions of people in the West), I have not found in the data any significant effect of the rate of change as opposed to the level of industrial production.

2

The Basic Mechanisms

Having reviewed the basic facts, let me turn to the mechanisms. I see the transition as being shaped by two main mechanisms. The first is *reallocation*. A typical description of what happened at the beginning of transition is that price liberalization and the removal of subsidies triggered a collapse of state firms, and that growth in the new private sector was simply insufficient to take up the slack. I think that this description is basically right. But its logic is less straightforward than it first appears. Why was there such a collapse of state firms? Why, if the private sector was unable to grow fast enough, didn't existing firms keep producing until new firms could appear? I discuss these issues in Section 2.1. In that context, I discuss the idea that part of the decrease in activity was due not so much to reallocation or reorganization, but rather to *disorganization*. The idea that transition has been associated with disorganization sounds plausible enough. The issue is of what exactly it means, and how we should think about it. I take this issue up in Section 2.2.

The second basic mechanism, which has played an increasing role as time has passed, is *restructuring*. It is one of the reasons why output growth since the start of the recovery has been associated primarily with increases in productivity rather than with decreases in unemployment. It implies important interactions between growth and unemployment. Faster restructuring can lead to higher unemployment. Higher unemployment can in turn slow down restructuring. I take up these issues in Section 2.3.

The reader will note the lack of emphasis in this book on the role of macroeconomic—monetary and fiscal—policies. This is for two reasons. The first is that I do not think that the basic, U-shaped, evolution of output in these countries is primarily the result of macroeconomic policies. The second is that, despite the pronouncements by some that tight policies were responsible for the output decline, and the pronouncements by others that stabilization has been the key to recovery, I feel we are some way from understanding the effects of macroeconomic policies in the context of transition economies. I discuss these issues at more length, but admittedly without resolution, in Section 2.4.

2.1 Reallocation

Think of the pre-transition economy as dominated by state firms, producing mediocre goods. Think of transition as allowing for the production of better goods by new, private, firms. Think of reallocation as the process through which resources, capital and labour, are reallocated to the production of these better goods. The question is: Under what circumstances will reallocation lead to a period of output decline and higher unemployment?

To answer this, let me start with the simplest two-sector model I can think of.[1] Think of two sectors, a 'state sector', producing mediocre goods ('state goods' for short), and a 'private sector', producing better goods ('private goods' for short). What I have in mind here is a distinction based on the type of goods produced, not based on ownership distinctions. Index variables in the state sector by s, variables in the private sector by p.

Assume that the two goods are produced according to identical constant returns production functions, $Y_i = F(N_i, K_i)$, where Y_i, N_i, K_i denote output, employment and capital in sector $i = s, p$. Assume the two goods to be perfect substitutes, up to a quality differential: one private good is worth $(1 + \theta)$ state goods, $\theta > 0$. The assumption of perfect substitutability makes the analytics much easier; it is not essential.

Obviously, in an economy without distortions, only private goods would be produced. Assume that pre-transition, however, most goods are state goods. More specifically, assume that a proportion ε of capital and labour is used in the private sector, and a proportion $(1 - \varepsilon)$ is used in the state sector. As the mnemonic ε suggests, think of private production as a small proportion of total output.

Ignore for the time being the details of how this distorted allocation was actually achieved under central planning. Simply assume that this distorted allocation is sustained through a combination of subsidies—explicit or implicit— to state firms and taxes—again, explicit or implicit—on private firms.

Let σ be the rate of subsidy and τ be the tax rate. The assumption of perfect substitutability up to a differential implies a simple relation between σ, τ, and θ, the quality differential. For buyers to be willing to buy both goods, the prices of the two goods must reflect the quality differential. Thus, if we denote the prices of the two goods by P_s and P_p, then it must be that $P_p = (1 + \theta)P_s$. For firms to be willing to produce either good, the after subsidy/tax prices to firms must be the same. Thus, $(1 + \sigma)P_s = (1 - \tau)P_p$. Putting the two relations together implies

$$\frac{1+\sigma}{1-\tau} = (1+\theta). \tag{1.1}$$

The combination of taxes and subsidies pre-transition must be such that buyers are willing to buy mediocre goods, and state firms are willing to produce them.

Denote the wage by W, and the real wage (say, in terms of private goods) by $w \equiv W/P_p$. Taking capital as fixed in the short run in each sector, we can write the demand functions for labour in the state sector and the private sector pre-transition as

$$N_s = K_s f\left(\frac{W}{P_s(1+\sigma)}\right) = K_s f\left(\frac{w(1+\theta)}{(1+\sigma)}\right), \qquad (1.2)$$

and

$$N_p = K_p f\left(\frac{W}{P_p(1-\tau)}\right) = K_p f\left(\frac{w}{1-\tau}\right). \qquad (1.3)$$

The equilibrium pre-transition is characterized in Figure 2.1. The real wage is measured on the vertical axis. The demand for labour by state firms, SS, is measured going left to right on the horizontal axis. The demand for labour by private firms, PP, is measured going right to left. Assume that the initial equilibrium is at point A, where there is no unemployment. A proportion ε of employment (and capital) is in the private sector, $(1 - \varepsilon)$ in the state sector. The equilibrium real wage is given by w.

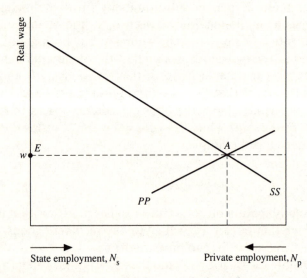

Fig. 2.1. Production in the state and the private sector pre-transition

Although there is no unemployment, the economy, which mostly produces mediocre state goods, is clearly inefficient. Let Y^* be the efficient level of output, the level which would prevail if capital and labour were employed only in the production of private goods (so that the economy was at point E in Figure 2.1). It follows from the above assumptions that the ratio of output to its efficient level is given by:

$$\frac{Y}{Y^*} = \frac{(1-\varepsilon)+\varepsilon(1+\theta)}{1+\theta} = \frac{1+\varepsilon\theta}{1+\theta}.$$

If, for example, ε is equal to 0.2 and $\theta = 1$ (so that private goods are twice as valuable as state goods), the economy is operating at 60 per cent of its efficient level.

2.1.1 The effects of transition

Take transition to mean the elimination of subsidies to state firms and of taxes on private firms. Let me start with the assumption that there were only subsidies pre-transition and that these subsidies are removed. This assumption is important and I shall return to it when discussing results below.

The equilibrium after the removal of subsidies is characterized in Figure 2.2. From equation (1.2), the elimination of subsidies shifts the labour demand from SS to SS'. From equation (1.3), the demand for labour by private firms is unaffected, so that PP does not shift.[2] At a given real wage, the result is a decrease in state employment, no change in private sector employment, and thus an increase in unemployment from 0 to U. As long as the real wage does not decline to w, transition leads to an initial increase in unemployment.[3]

Since output decreases in the state sector and remains unchanged in the private sector, total output also clearly goes down. What happens to utility depends on the relation between the real wage and the marginal utility of leisure. If the real wage is equal to the marginal utility of leisure, then the elimination of subsidies leads the economy to return to

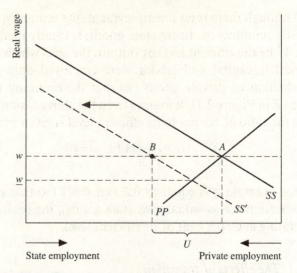

Fig. 2.2. The effects of removing subsidies on state employment, private employment, and unemployment

its first best level (given the initial allocation of capital in both sectors) and thus improves utility. If, at the opposite extreme, the marginal utility of leisure is equal to 0, then utility moves with output and thus obviously goes down.

What happens over time to employment depends on what happens to both the real wage and the interest rate. Consider the admittedly extreme assumption that both remain unchanged. The removal of subsidies leads to a decrease in the after-subsidy marginal product of capital in the state sector, and thus to capital decumulation over time. Given that factor prices determine the capital–labour ratio and that factor prices are fixed by assumption here, capital decumulation implies a proportional decrease in state employment over time. Since there is no change in the marginal product of capital in the private sector, there is no change in capital accumulation and thus no change in private employment over time. In this extreme case, total employment keeps decreasing until the state sector has disappeared, and the unemployment rate is equal to state employment pre-transition. This case is extreme, but shows how, unless either real wages or interest rates decrease substantially, employment and output may decline for some time after the initial shock.[4]

I shall examine the fiscal implications of transition at more length in Chapter 4. But it is worth thinking about what happens to government revenues and expenditures within this simple model. On the one hand, the elimination of subsidies decreases government expenditures. On the other, if the government pays unemployment benefits, higher unemployment increases government expenditures. Can we be sure that the budget will improve? Not necessarily. Take the case we just looked at in which the elimination of subsidies eventually leads to the elimination of the state sector. Subsidies pre-transition are equal to $\sigma P_s Y_s$. From equation (1.1), and under the assumption that there are only subsidies pre-transition, the subsidy rate σ is equal to θ, so that $\sigma P_s Y_s = \theta P_s Y_s$. Let B be unemployment benefits per worker. After transition and the disappearance of the state sector, unemployment benefits are equal to BN_s, or equivalently $(B/W)WN_s$. Denote the share of labour in state production by $\alpha \equiv WN_S / P_s Y_s$. Then, transition leads to an improvement in the budget position if and only if the rate of subsidy is such that

$$\theta > \alpha \frac{B}{W}.$$

This condition may well fail. It is more likely to fail the lower the quality differential of private goods, the higher the share of labour in production, and the higher the ratio of unemployment benefits to the wage (the 'replacement rate'). If it fails, the elimination of subsidies leads to a deterioration of the budget. The condition was derived under extreme assumptions, but the warning is general: the decrease in subsidies may not lead to an improvement in the budget.

2.1.2 Open questions

It would seem as if we have a simple explanation for the U-shaped response of output and employment I documented in Chapter 1: removing the subsidies to state firms can lead to a decrease in output and employment, which can build for some time before turning around. But there are at least two loose ends in the argument: the assumption that wages do not decline enough to avoid unemployment, and the assumption that transition can be thought of primarily as the removal of subsidies to state firms rather than the removal of taxes and other restrictions on private firms. Let's take both issues in turn.

(1) The question of why wages don't adjust sufficiently to avoid unemployment really has two parts. First, subsidies had to be financed in some way pre-transition. To the extent that the elimination of subsidies comes with a reduction in the effective taxation of labour income, why don't workers accept a reduction in (pre-tax) wages? Second, why doesn't unemployment lead workers to accept a reduction in the real wage? I shall spend much of the next chapter discussing wage and employment determination during transition, in both state and private firms. I shall, at this stage, just look at the aggregate data. This is done in Figures 2.3 and 2.4.

Figure 2.3 gives the evolution of the *consumption wage*, the nominal wage divided by the CPI. Figure 2.4 gives the evolution of the *product wage*, the nominal wage divided by the GDP deflator.[5] In the model above, these two measures would be the same. In the real world, because in particular of the difference between the compositions of consumption and of GDP (in particular, the larger weight of food and housing in consumption, and the presence of imported goods in consumption but not in GDP) they can move differently. And indeed, in Central Europe, they very much have. The consumption wage can be constructed from 1988 on. The product wage can only be constructed from 1989 on

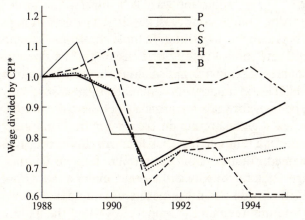

Fig. 2.3. The evolution of the consumption wage
* Value in 1988=1

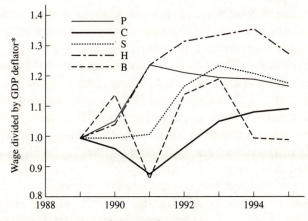

Fig. 2.4. The evolution of the product wage
* Value in 1989=1

(there is no reliable GDP deflator for 1988). In the two figures, I give the evolutions of the real wage in calendar time, rather than in years since beginning of transition as in Chapter 1.

Figure 2.3 shows a clear decline in the consumption

wage.[6] The consumption wage is below its 1988 value for all countries. In most countries, the largest decline took place at the beginning of transition. In most countries, consumption wages are now stable or increasing. The exception is Bulgaria, where consumption wages have kept declining and stood, in 1995, at only 60 per cent of their 1988 level.

The relevant wage for firms however is the product wage. Figure 2.4 gives a rather different story from Figure 2.3: the product wage has increased in four out of five countries (and remained roughly constant in the fifth, Bulgaria). This suggests that, while we still need to understand why—and I shall try to do so in the next two chapters—the working assumption made in the model above that the real product wage was constant has not been too bad an approximation to reality.[7]

(2) The discussion above was based on the assumption that liberalization was associated with a removal of subsidies. But if, as has indeed been the case, liberalization implies both a decrease in subsidies to state firms and the removal of restrictions and taxes on new private firms, the outcome is less clear-cut. From equations (1.2) and (1.3), and if both σ and τ were positive pre-transition, transition is associated with an adverse shift in labour demand by the state sector, a shift to the left of SS, but also a favourable shift in labour demand by the private sector, a shift to the left of PP. The effect on employment, and thus on unemployment, at a given wage, is ambiguous. As a matter of logic, there is no compelling reason why transition should have been associated with a large decrease in employment.[8]

How serious an issue is this? After all, one might argue that, while it could have turned out different, the main effect of liberalization was an adverse shift of the demand for labour by state firms rather than a favourable shift of the private demand for labour, and thus a large increase in unemployment. Table 2.1 shows that transition was indeed associated with a large decline in explicit subsidies to state

Table 2.1. The evolution of subsidies
to state firms (percentage of GDP)

	1989	1993
Bulgaria	15.5	4.8
Czech Republic	25.0	4.4
Slovak Republic	25.0	4.8
Hungary	12.1	4.1
Poland	12.9	3.0

Source: IMF [1994, tables 14 and 15].

firms between 1989 and 1993. And, as I shall discuss in the next chapter, this decline was associated, for the most part, with a decrease in implicit subsidies and a tightening of state firms' budget constraints.

But this table only tells half of the story. Surely, transition was also associated with the elimination of restrictions on the development of private firms, through the lifting of either prohibitive taxation or legal restrictions. Why was the net effect on employment negative? I now want to argue that state firms were affected by more than just the decrease in subsidies and price liberalization; that, especially at the beginning, transition was associated with disorganization, and that disorganization accounts for some of the decrease in activity. I develop this theme in the next section.

2.2 Disorganization

I have so far treated the pre-transition economy as if it was a market economy with distortions. While one can indeed map the restrictions that firms were facing pre-transition in terms of shadow taxes and subsidies, the fact is that pre-transition economies were not market economies . . . They were organized differently, around a central plan rather than around markets. Transition destroyed that organization. And, I now argue, this accounts for some of the output decline at the beginning of transition.

The notion that systemic changes can lead to lower output for a while is plausible enough. Indeed it is a frequent, if somewhat vague, theme in the literature on transition that economists have not paid enough attention to the implications of systemic changes. I want to explore one specific channel through which this may happen. It may not be the only one, but it strikes me as having played an important role in the early part of transition.[9]

When central planning ended, production in the state sector was organized around bilateral relations between state firms. Typically, firms had or knew of only one supplier for each input, of one buyer for each output. Such a structure can easily lead to large disruptions in production: if, for any reason, this supplier does not deliver, production may come to a stop. Under central planning, the presence of the central planner was enough to avoid most of these problems; through threats and bribes, the planner could induce firms to deliver most goods most of the time. Once the central planner disappeared, these problems came to the fore. The result was a set of disruptions in production and trade, or what can be thought of quite generally as *disorganization*.[10]

2.2.1 An example

Let me take the above argument further by developing a simple model. Think of an economy just after transition, just after central planning has disappeared. Think of a state firm which needs n inputs in order to produce. If all inputs are available, the firm can produce n units of output. Otherwise, output is equal to 0. The parameter n can be taken as a measure of the complexity of production in the state sector.

Each input is supplied by one supplier only. This captures the specificity of relations between firms inherited from central planning. Each supplier has an alternative use for his input, with value c. Think of c as a private sector alternative. Pre-transition, c may well have been equal to 0 for most suppliers. Think of transition as leading to an increase in c: transition allows suppliers to consider alternative uses, from small-scale own-production, to the sale of the input to a foreign buyer, and so on.

This structure implies that the state firm faces n bargaining problems, one with each of its suppliers. State firm production will take place only if the firm can convince each one to supply. Why might bargaining fail even when it is efficient to produce in the state firm? One reason may be asymmetric information: the firm may not know what alternative opportunities each supplier has; suppliers may try to bluff and ask for a high price for their input; the firm in turn may refuse to pay. This is the route I shall follow here.

Think of the suppliers as having different alternatives, and of these alternatives as being private information. More formally, assume that c is distributed uniformly on $[0, \bar{c}]$. Let $F(.)$ denote the distribution function, so that $F(0) = 0$ and $F(\bar{c}) = 1$. Draws are independent across suppliers. The distribution of c is known, but the specific realization of each c is private information to each supplier. Finally, think of the state firm as announcing a take-it-or-leave-it price p to each supplier (given the symmetry built into the assumptions, the price is the same for all suppliers). If the price exceeds the reservation prices of all suppliers, production takes place in the state firm. Otherwise, it does not, and all suppliers use their own private opportunity.

Given these assumptions, we can characterize expected state, private, and total production as a function of $\bar{c}$ and n. The first step is to solve for the profit-maximizing price set by the state firm. Given price p, expected profit is given by

$$\pi = (F(p))^n (1 - p)n.$$

The first term is the probability that production takes place. The second is equal to profit (the output price minus the input price, times the number of inputs) if production takes place. Maximizing with respect to p yields the profit-maximizing price

$$p = \min(\overline{c}, \frac{n}{n+1}).$$

The state firm never pays more than the maximum alternative opportunity, $\overline{c}$. But, if the maximum alternative opportunity exceeds $(n/(n+1))$, the firm does not increase its price. Increasing the price would increase the probability that production takes place, but would decrease expected profit.

Given this price, expected state production, Y_s, is equal to

$$Y_s = n\min(1, (\frac{n}{n+1}\frac{1}{\overline{c}})^n).$$

Expected private production, Y_p, is equal to the probability that state production does not take place times the conditional expected sum of alternative opportunities (conditional on at least one private alternative being larger than the price offered by the state firm). With some manipulations, Y_p can be written as

$$Y_p = \frac{n\overline{c}}{2}\max(0, 1-(\frac{n}{n+1}\frac{1}{\overline{c}})^{n+1}).$$

Expected total production is in turn equal to

$$Y \equiv Y_s + Y_p.$$

The best way to see what these equations imply is to look at Figure 2.5, which plots the behaviour, for $n = 4$, of expected state, private, and total production (all three normalized by the number of inputs, n) for values of $\overline{c}$ ranging from 0.4 to 2.4.

To interpret the figure, keep the efficient benchmark in mind. This efficient outcome would prevail if, for example, the state firm knew the alternative opportunities of each supplier and thus paid each one its alternative opportunity,

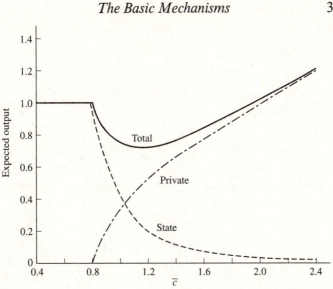

Fig. 2.5. Expected state, private, and total output ($n = 4$)

or if there were markets for inputs which revealed these alternative opportunities. So long as $\bar{c}$ was less than 1, production would always take place in the state sector. As $\bar{c}$ increased above 1, it would sometimes be efficient not to produce in the state sector: expected production in the state sector would decrease, but total production would increase. Eventually, as $\bar{c}$ became very large, most production would take place in the private sector, with expected total production increasing linearly with $\bar{c}$. In other words, an increase in $\bar{c}$ would lead to a decrease in state production, but to an unambiguous increase in total production.

In contrast to this efficient outcome, increases in private opportunities lead here, at least initially, to such a large decrease in state production that the net effect is a decrease in total production. As Figure 2.5 shows, total production starts declining when $\bar{c}$ exceeds $n/(n+1) = 0.8$. For $\bar{c}$ equal to 1.0, the efficient outcome would be that production still only takes place in the state firm, with total production equal to n (1 in the figure, as output is divided by the number of

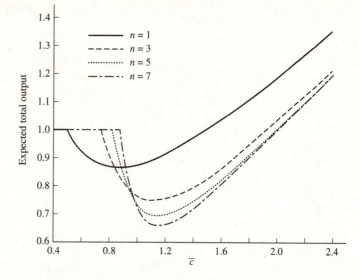

Fig. 2.6. Expected total output for different values of n

inputs). The actual outcome is a production level of only 0.75. It is not before $\bar{c}$ has reached a value of about 2.0 that total production is again equal to its pre-transition level.[11]

Complexity of production in the state sector increases the size of the decline in output. Figure 2.6 shows the effects of alternative values of n on the evolution of expected total production (again normalized by the number of inputs) as a function of $\bar{c}$. The larger n, the higher the price that the state firm offers. Thus, the higher n, the higher the value of $\bar{c}$ required to trigger the collapse of the state sector. But, also the higher n, the smaller the probability that production takes place in the state firm for $\bar{c} \geq n/(n+1)$, and thus the greater the initial collapse of total production as $\bar{c}$ increases. As n approaches infinity, the price offered by the state firm approaches 1, and state production collapses as soon as $\bar{c}$ increases above 1: the probability that at least one supplier will have a realization of c greater than 1 goes to 1.

Putting these results into words: pre-transition, suppliers have such poor alternative opportunities that the state firm can offer a price at which there is no better alternative than to supply. As transition starts, and alternatives improve, some suppliers now have more attractive opportunities. Not knowing which suppliers are bluffing and which are not, the state firm has no choice other than to offer a given price and take the risk of not getting the inputs. The result can be an initial collapse in state production, and a decrease in total production, triggered by the improvement in private opportunities.

2.2.2 Extensions

The example we have just seen suggests two reasons why transition was associated with an initial decline in output and employment in the state sector, apart from the effects of price liberalization and the elimination of subsidies I focused on in the previous section. The first was the disappearance of the central planner, and the sheer problems of organizing production without it. Markets could not do the job overnight. The second was the very appearance of new private opportunities, making state production even more prone to bargaining failures, and thus to collapse. Indeed, this example suggests that part of the state sector collapse may have been due to the improvement in private sector opportunities.

Let me now develop aspects of this general theme further. The problem of the state firm in our example comes from the inability of the firm and its suppliers to divide efficiently the rents from production. As such, the argument is a special case of a more general argument, that inefficient rent-grabbing explains important features of transition. For example, Shleifer and Vishny [1993] have argued, in the context of Russia, that political decentralization has led to competition among rent-seekers—be they politicians, building inspectors, and so on—with large adverse effects on the growth of the new private sector.[12] To take another example, I shall argue in the next chapter that restructuring in state firms has also been hampered by the inability to divide rents from restructuring efficiently. Most of the rent-seeking arguments have focused, however, more on the obstacles to growth than on the initial decline in state firms. Disorganization can potentially explain the initial decline as well.

Problems of specificity may have been acute at the beginning of transition. But they are not altogether absent in Western economies. For some goods, markets eliminate the scope for bargaining altogether. In many cases, however, goods are sufficiently specific that markets are not the solution and firms have to engage in bilateral relations. One of the ways they avoid some of the inefficiencies shown in the example above is through long-term relations.[13] The prospect of repeated interactions in the future gives both sides an incentive to be more truthful, to achieve a more efficient outcome today. Interestingly, transition is precisely the type of environment in which long-term relations can only play a limited role: suppliers who know that state firms will either close or, at least, restructure and change many of their suppliers may have little incentive to behave other than opportunistically.

In many Central and Eastern European countries, transition was preceded by a slow decline in output, which accelerated just pre-transition. The argument above suggests an explanation. Once state firms started expecting central planning to come to an end, they had less reason to care about threats of future punishment by the central planner, or about maintaining good relations with other firms. The result was more frequent failures by firms to deliver, more disruptions, and a decrease in production even before transition had officially started.

The role that disorganization played in the initial decline in output is obviously difficult to quantify, and much of the evidence can only be suggestive. I shall limit myself to a few remarks here and refer the reader to a longer discussion in Blanchard and Kremer [1997].

Perhaps the most suggestive evidence comes from the

Table 2.2. Trade between Central European countries and between Central European countries and the former Soviet Union (percentage change in dollar terms)

	1989	1990	1991	1992	1993
Exports to other CE	−8.4	−25.1	−20.1	−9.7	−13.1
Imports from other CE	−8.9	−17.3	−25.8	−4.4	−10.5
Exports to FSU	−9.3	−16.1	−25.1	−31.7	16.0
Imports from FSU	−12.5	−10.8	−9.3	−6.5	1.3

Note: 'CE' stands for Central Europe; 'FSU' stands for the former Soviet Union. The first two lines only differ because of measurement and reporting errors.

Source: EBRD [1994, table 8.2].

effects of what has been called the 'CMEA shock'. In early 1991, the previous system of trade between Central and Eastern European countries was officially abandoned.[14] The outcome was a near-collapse of trade. (This scenario was repeated one year later with the independence and the collapse of trade among the republics of the former Soviet Union.) Numbers on exports and imports from and to Central Europe, for 1989 to 1993, are presented in Table 2.2.[15]

Why was there such a collapse of trade, especially within Central Europe (where foreign exchange restrictions were irrelevant from 1991 on)? Disorganization of trade sounds plausible here. To go further would require an assessment of how much of the decrease in trade can be explained by more conventional factors. This has not been done yet.

Another way of assessing the relevance of disorganization is to look at the evolution of a measure of reported shortages of materials by firms, both over time and across countries. This measure has three merits. First, it is available, for a number of countries and years. Second, it is plausibly correlated with disorganization. Third, shortages are not a natural implication of most alternative theories of output decline.[16]

Table 2.3. Percentage of firms experiencing shortages of materials

	min.	max.	1996(1) value
Czech Republic 1993(1)–96(1)	3	9	5
Hungary 1992(1)–96(1)	6	11	5
Poland 1993(3)–96(1)	3	6	5
Bulgaria 1993(1)–96(1)	15	33	25
Romania 1992(1)–96(1)	8	39	15
Latvia 1993(1)–96(1)	21	32	21
Lithuania 1993(3)–96(1)	13	43	17

Source: OECD [1996, business survey annex].

Table 2.3 gives the evidence for a number of Central European and Baltic countries. The strength of these data is that they come from roughly identical surveys across countries. Their drawback is that the surveys were put in place only in 1992 or 1993, and thus do not cover the early period of transition, where disorganization is likely to have been relatively more important.

I draw two conclusions from this table. First, in the Czech Republic, Hungary, and Poland, shortages of materials have played a very limited role since 1992–3. The current numbers are comparable in magnitude to those obtained from similar surveys of firms in Western Europe.[17] Second, the evidence from those Central European countries which are doing less well suggests a larger role for disorganization. In Bulgaria and Romania, two of the countries with the largest drop in output, supply shortages still played an important role more than two years after the beginning of transition. The same is true of the Baltic states. Evidence from surveys of firms for Russia and the new Republics shows that shortages have typically played a more important role there than in Central Europe.[18]

This suggests one proximate reason why the output decline

has been substantially more pronounced in Eastern than in Central Europe. In Russia, for example, the collapse of state production happened even before subsidies had been substantially reduced (subsidies, as measured by the EBRD, were up in Russia in 1993 compared to 1989). One reason may be that disorganization has played a much more important role. Why? One can think of a number of plausible explanations. Specificities may well have been higher in many of the republics of the Soviet Union than in, say, Poland or the Czech Republic, leading to a larger collapse of both intra- and inter-republican trade. Distance from the West, and thus the volume of trade and the scope for foreign firms to come in and alleviate problems of specificity, may also have played an important role.

Having gone out on a limb, let me go even further and speculate about the different evolutions of output in Central Europe and in China. The analysis so far suggests at least two differences. Most of the liberalization in China has taken the form of a decrease in restrictions on the private sector, rather than a decrease in the subsidies to state firms. The analysis in Section 2.1 suggests that, by itself, this is more likely to lead to an increase in employment and output. Second, the ability of the Chinese government to maintain political control implies that centralized allocation has not been fully replaced by decentralized bargaining. And third, China's commitment to maintain state firms, using subsidies if necessary, may have lengthened horizons, allowing for a larger role of long-term relations between firms and their suppliers, and thus avoiding the collapse of state firms in the face of new private opportunities.

2.3 Restructuring

I have focused so far on reallocation. There is another important dimension to transition, namely the restructuring of state firms. If they are to survive at all, state firms must change in fundamental ways. This means not only changes in the structure of their ownership, but also changes in the structure and the organization of their production.

The flaws and inefficiencies of state firms had been well documented pre-transition, and studies of specific sectors and firms post-transition have largely confirmed the previous diagnosis.[19] Because of the incentives created by central planning, state firms were too large (and too few). They were too vertically integrated (in order to protect themselves against disruptions in supply, and thus with motivations different from those that lead to vertical integration in the West). The products were of poor quality. Capital intensity was high compared to firms in the West, but the technology embodied in that capital was typically behind that of firms in the West. There was considerable hoarding of inputs, including labour.

Thus, if they are to survive at all, state firms must restructure. They must redefine their product line, close those plants which are no longer needed and lay off the workers in those plants. They must reduce labour hoarding. They must replace many of their managers, those who do not have the skills to manage firms in a market economy. They must replace most of their capital, or at least most of their equipment.[20]

From a macroeconomic point of view, restructuring has two main implications. On the one hand, it increases productivity and output. On the other hand, it may lead, for some time, to a decrease in employment, and thus an increase in unemployment. Let me examine these effects more closely.

2.3.1 *Restructuring, productivity, and employment*

Under what conditions will restructuring in the state sector lead to an initial decrease in state sector employment? Under what conditions will it lead to a decrease in overall employment? For how long?

The question of how productivity improvements in one

sector affect employment in that sector and employment in the economy as a whole is an old question in economics. The modern answer dates back at least to Baumol [1967] and has recently been revisited in a general equilibrium context by Cohen and Saint-Paul [1995]. It goes as follows.

Employment in the sector will go down if the demand for the output of the sector is sufficiently inelastic. The standard example here is agriculture, where productivity growth has led to steady decreases in employment over time. By assuming that state goods and private goods were perfect substitutes, I excluded this possibility in the two-sector model I introduced in Section 2.1, but let me explore its implications briefly here. If the elasticity of substitution between state and private goods is low enough, the demand for state goods will be inelastic. An increase in productivity will lead to an increase in output, but not by enough to avoid a decrease in employment in the state sector. What will happen to employment in the private sector? At a given real consumption wage, the price of state goods will allow private firms to pay their workers less in terms of private goods. The demand for labour in the private sector will therefore go up. Whether it will go up by enough to offset the decrease in employment in the state sector is ambiguous; it depends on the elasticity of the demand for labour in the private sector. To summarize, if the elasticity of substitution between state and private goods is low enough, restructuring will lead to a decrease in state employment. It may, but it need not, also lead to a decrease in overall employment.

Alternatively, employment will go down if technological progress is labour-saving and the elasticity between capital and labour is sufficiently low. This is the route I shall follow here. Suppose that the production function for the state sector is given by

$$Y_s = F((1 + \theta)N_s, K_s). \tag{3.1}$$

Think of restructuring as leading to an increase in θ, a decrease in the amount of labour needed to produce a given

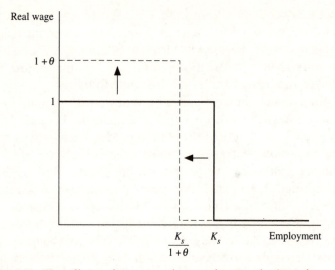

Fig. 2.7. The effects of restructuring on the marginal product of labour

amount of output. An example would be the elimination of labour hoarding. Then, if the elasticity of substitution between labour and capital is low, restructuring will lead, at a given real wage, to a decrease in employment.

The easiest way to see this is to consider the limiting, Leontief, case. Assume that, with proper choice of units, the production function is given by $Y_s = \min((1 + \theta)N_s, K_s)$. And take restructuring to lead to an increase in θ from 0 to some positive value. This increase in θ will shift labour demand as shown in Figure 2.7. For real wages less than or equal to 1, labour demand will decrease from K_s to $K_s/(1 + \theta)$. For real wages between 1 and $(1 + \theta)$, labour demand will increase from 0 to $K_s/(1 + \theta)$. Thus, if the state firm was initially employing as many workers as could be employed given capital, employment will unambiguously go down.

Let me incorporate this treatment of restructuring of the state sector into the two-sector model of Section 2.1. Let me go away from the Leontief case, and draw labour demand in

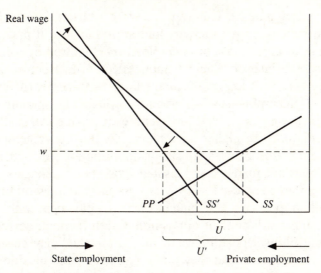

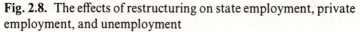

Fig. 2.8. The effects of restructuring on state employment, private employment, and unemployment

the state sector as the smooth curve *SS* in Figure 2.8. Let *PP* represent, as before, labour demand in the private sector. Both demand curves are drawn after the elimination of taxes and subsidies, and unemployment is equal to *U*. What happens when state firms start restructuring? Assume that restructuring leads to an increase in θ in equation (3.1). As long as the elasticity of substitution between capital and labour is low, the effect of restructuring will be to twist labour demand from *SS* to *SS'*.[21] At the initial real wage, state employment will decrease, private employment will remain the same, and unemployment will therefore increase.

Over time, employment will increase in the state sector. This is because, at a given real wage, an increase in θ leads to an increase in the rate of return on capital in state firms. State firms will thus accumulate capital (or at least accumulate more capital than they would otherwise have done). As capital increases, the demand for labour by state firms will shift to the right, reducing unemployment.

To summarize, at a given real wage, restructuring leads to an increase in productivity and in output. But it may also lead to an increase in unemployment, followed by a faster decrease later on. These dynamic effects of restructuring are the source of important interactions between restructuring and unemployment, interactions which are shaping the transition. As we have just seen, restructuring can lead, for some time, to higher unemployment. But high unemployment in turn may lead to strong opposition to restructuring. Unless adequately compensated, workers or managers who feel they may lose their job as a result of the restructuring will oppose it. The higher the unemployment rate, the stronger will be their opposition. Given the high degree of control insiders still have in state firms, they may be—and the evidence is that they often have been—in a position to prevent restructuring.

Outsider privatization would seem to be the natural solution. Once outsiders own the firm, they will restructure if it is efficient to do so, whether or not this leads to an initial reduction in employment. But this advice assumes rather than gives the solution. For the same reason they oppose restructuring, insiders will oppose—and indeed often successfully have opposed—outsider privatization, either at the political level or at the level of the firm.

How restructuring and unemployment interact, and how this interaction depends in turn on the mode of privatization, the ability of firms to compensate those who lose their job, the benefits given to the unemployed, and so on, will be one of the main topics I take up in the next two chapters. But a basic implication should be clear already. Countries which had a large initial shock and thus a large increase in unemployment are likely to restructure more slowly. This may limit a further increase in unemployment, but it will also slow down the recovery. This may explain, for example, why Bulgaria, which had one of the largest initial output declines in Central Europe, is also one of the countries which have the slowest recovery.

2.4 Macroeconomic Policies

How much of the movement in output can be explained not by the factors I have focused on so far, but rather by shifts in aggregate demand? Some have argued that much of the output decline can be blamed on excessively tight macroeconomic policies (for example, Laski 1993). Others have argued that the empirical evidence points instead to the opposite conclusion, that macroeconomic stabilization has been the key to output recovery (for example, Bruno and Easterly 1995). Both claims are too strong. Macroeconomic policies should neither get too much of the blame for the output decline, nor too much of the credit for the recovery.

There is broad agreement about the effects of demand policies in Western economies. Put roughly, and omitting all the standard caveats, exchange rate and monetary policies which lead to depreciation or to low real interest rates are thought to increase output over its equilibrium path for some time. And so are fiscal expansions.

The effects of these policies may, however, be quite different in transition economies. This is for two reasons. The first is familiar from the discussion of high inflations. If and when macroeconomic policies lead to high inflation, inflation itself is likely to have adverse effects on output. The second is more specific to transition economies. Macroeconomic policies are likely not only to affect output around its equilibrium path, but also to affect this equilibrium path in important ways. Here, what happens depends very much on the behaviour of state firms, an issue I touched upon in the previous section, and to which I shall return at more length in the next chapter.

Take exchange rate policies for example. Exchange rate policies which lead to a large undervaluation—as was typically the case early in transition[22]—lead, other things being equal, to a larger trade surplus and an increase in demand. But a large undervaluation may also allow state firms to avoid restructuring for some time. This in turn may lead to less employment decline in the short run, but less output and employment growth later on.

Take monetary policy. If money growth comes in part from refinancing bad loans or bailing out banks with bad portfolios, the effects of an increase in money growth on investment will be small. They may indeed be perverse: the anticipation of future bail-outs of bad loans to state firms may lead banks to lend to state rather than to new private firms. If, in turn, state firms borrow to maintain employment rather than to finance investment, the effect of anticipated bail-outs may well be to reduce overall investment.

Finally, take fiscal policy. To the extent that a fiscal deficit reflects subsidies to state firms, it may also slow down restructuring, thus leading to more employment now, but less output and employment in the future.[23]

What has been the actual stance of exchange rate, monetary, and fiscal policy in transition economies? Is there evidence that tighter policies have been associated with a larger/smaller output decline, a stronger/weaker output recovery? I do not think we have a clear answer at this point.

Figure 2.9(a) shows the heterogeneity of inflation experiences even within Central Europe. As with the figures in Chapter 1, year 0 is the year before transition for each country. Inflation is measured using the CPI. In two countries, Poland and Bulgaria, transition was associated with a large adjustment of prices, and thus a short period of high inflation.[24] In two countries, the Czech and the Slovak Republics (only one country at the time), the initial effect on inflation was much smaller. And in Hungary, it was practically non-existent. Since then, inflation has stabilized in four of the five countries, although at quite different levels. Poland and Hungary's inflation rates are around 25 per cent, the Czech and Slovak republics' around 10 per cent. In Bulgaria, inflation has recently started increasing.

Figure 2.9(b) (which replicates Figure 1.1 in Chapter 1) plots the behaviour of output in the five countries. A

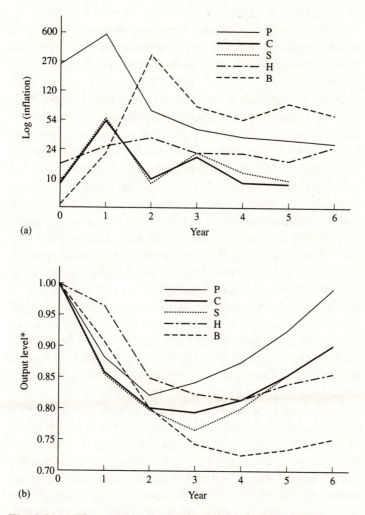

Fig. 2.9(a). The evolution of CPI inflation; **2.9(b).** The evolution of GDP

* Value in the year before transition = 1.0

comparison of Figures 2.9(a) and 2.9(b) does not suggest obvious correlations between the output decline/recovery and the level of change in inflation. There is little evidence that those countries which have either avoided the burst of initial inflation, or decreased inflation more, or which now have a lower rate of inflation, have done better in terms of output.

In the recent past, a number of papers have looked at the relation between inflation and output across all countries in transition, rather than only the five countries I have just looked at. Their conclusions are stronger than those suggested by Figure 2.9. De Melo *et al.* [1995] find that countries which have had a lower average rate of inflation since the beginning of transition have also had a smaller output decline. Fischer *et al.* [1996] find that countries which had a lower average rate of inflation from 1992 to 1994 also had a higher rate of growth of output over the same period. There can be little doubt that very high inflation has large adverse effects on output. In 1992, ten of the twelve CIS countries had annual inflation rates above 1,000 per cent; this was still the case for nine of them in 1993, and for seven of them in 1994. Beyond that, it is not clear what one should make of these correlations. Do these results tell us about the effects of stabilization—or the lack of stabilization—on the behaviour of output, or about the effects of the output decline on money growth and inflation? Could stabilization be a proxy of the broader set of measures taken or not taken by the government? Lack of stabilization in Georgia, for example, is surely not the primary cause of the output decline. The civil war is, and is also the main cause of inflation. Åslund *et al.* [1996] show for example that, when one controls for the presence of a civil war and for initial membership in the rouble zone, there is no longer a significant relation between the output decline and average inflation across countries in transition.

To assess the role of aggregate demand in general, and the role of demand policies in particular, in the output decline and recovery, there is no substitute for looking at the various dimensions of policy in each country and estimating their effects on activity. Despite much work, the contribution of macroeconomic policies to the output decline and recovery in each country is still largely terra incognita. I shall take this state of affairs as an excuse to simply state my beliefs at this point.

Based in particular on work with Andrew Berg on Poland (Berg and Blanchard 1994) I have no doubt that aggregate demand played a role in the initial decline in output in Poland. How else to explain the decline in nearly all sectors at the beginning of transition?[25] Research on other Central European countries suggests the same conclusion: the general pattern of decline across sectors in the first few years of transition suggests the presence of a general shift in aggregate demand in addition to the relative demand shifts suggested by reallocation.[26]

Based on what we know about the behaviour of state firms, I also believe that tight policies may have hastened the process of restructuring and the recovery of output in a number of countries. At the same time, the general pattern of output decline and recovery appears too similar across countries, in light of the diversity of policies, to be primarily attributable to those policies. I realize that these are not very strong conclusions. But I do not feel confident to take a stronger stance at this point.

2.5 Conclusions

I have argued in this chapter that transition has been dominated by two main mechanisms, reallocation and restructuring. Reallocation (including one of its incarnations, disorganization) explains why transition was initially associated with higher unemployment. Restructuring can explain why the output recovery has been associated in large part with increases in productivity, and so far only limited gains in employment. In the next chapter, I want to look at some of the pieces of these mechanisms in more detail, from the initial reaction of state firms, to the nature of restructuring decisions, to the role of unemployment in the transition.

NOTES

1. This two-sector model is a close cousin of those used to study the effects of trade liberalization. See, for example, Mussa [1986]; Neary [1982]. One of the first uses of a two-sector model to discuss transition was in Flemming [1993]. The numerical general equilibrium model in Blanchard and Keeling [1996] parallels the discussion in this book by starting from a two-sector model, introducing one by one the various additional mechanisms described in this book, and discussing their effects on transition.

2. If we relax the assumption that state and private goods are perfect substitutes, the elimination of subsidies leads to an adverse shift of *both SS* and *PP*. At a given real consumption wage (the wage in terms of the consumption basket), employment is lower in both sectors. The reason for the adverse shift in the labour demand of private firms is the following: the elimination of subsidies leads to an increase in the price of state goods. To maintain a given real consumption wage requires an increase in the wage given the price of private goods. This increase in the wage in terms of private goods leads to a decrease in the demand for labour in the private sector. Thus, employment goes down at a given real consumption wage.

3. The value of w depends on the elasticities of substitution between capital and labour in production in both sectors. The lower the elasticity in the private sector, or the higher the elasticity in the state sector, the larger the decrease in the real wage required to avoid unemployment.

4. These dynamics are very similar to those characterized by Bruno and Sachs [1985] in response to an increase in the price

of oil in the presence of real wage rigidity. Under constant real wages and real interest rates, an increase in the price of oil leads the economy to implode as firms reduce their capital stock, and employment decreases in proportion.

5. I prefer to use the GDP deflator rather than the PPI. But the general picture would be similar if the PPI was used.

6. To the extent that there was rationing pre-transition, and that the quality of the goods has improved without being reflected in the index, it is more accurate to refer to this as a decline in the 'measured consumption wage'. What has happened to the true consumption wage has been hotly debated, but is inessential here.

7. The difference between the evolutions of the consumption wage and the product wage in Bulgaria is striking. While the consumption wage stands at only 60 per cent of its pre-transition level, the product wage shows little or no decline. As a matter of accounting, this reflects the fact that the CPI has increased by two-thirds relative to the GDP deflator. The increase in the CPI over the GDP deflator (and for that matter over the PPI) has been steady over the period. It is generally believed that at least part of the increase is spurious, and comes from underreporting of some of the prices which go into the construction of the PPI, which in turn is used in the construction of the GDP deflator. The dimension of the problem is, however, unknown.

8. I leave aside for the time being the notion that reallocation requires unemployment because workers have to go from one job to another. I shall elaborate on this later, but the numbers in Chapter 1 already make it clear that unemployment has been largely a stagnant pool, not the necessary byproduct of high churning.

9. What follows is based on Blanchard and Kremer [1997], which explores this idea at more length.

10. This argument is in contrast to *reorganization* theories of the output decline. These explore the idea that systemic changes make much of the existing stock of information obsolete. Rebuilding a new, appropriate, stock takes time, and during that time, measured output may well go down. In the model of Atkeson and Kehoe [1995], for example, transition allows firms to explore new and potentially better technologies. The

process of trial and error that they then go through leads to an initial decline in measured output, but also to the accumulation of information capital by firms. Eventually, measured output not only recovers, but exceeds its previous level. These theories clearly capture something. For example, the turnover rate of small private firms has been very high in most transition economies: many people try their skills at activities they could not engage in before, and many fail. But this mechanism has, I believe, little to do with the initial decline in output. The collapse of state firms surely does not come from them trying new ways, but rather from the opposite.

11. This example is closely related to the analysis by Murphy *et al.* [1992] of the effects of partial price liberalization. In their model, the fact that some prices are held fixed while others are left free can also lead to an inefficient diversion of output from state to private firms. In effect, the example here argues that the same outcome may happen even under full price liberalization.

12. Empirical evidence on the number and the size of bribes needed to run a business in Ukraine today is given by Kaufmann and Kaliberda [1995].

13. For a related discussion, see Greif and Kandel [1994].

14. See Rodrik [1994].

15. It would be better to give volume rather than dollar numbers. But I could not find a consistent set of volume numbers.

16. Shortages may reflect the effects of partial price liberalization, along the lines of Murphy *et al.* [1992]. In nearly all countries, however, prices have now been mostly liberalized, so that partial price liberalization plays a limited role in explaining shortages at this point. For a survey of progress on price liberalization as of 1995, see EBRD [1995].

17. Numbers from Berg and Blanchard [1994] show that, even in 1990 in Poland (the first year of transition), disruptions were not an important part of the story.

18. See Blanchard and Kremer [1997].

19. An excellent description of Polish firms in general, and of a number of state firms in particular, is given by Johnson and Loveman [1995]. Their description of Prochnik, a consumer clothing firm, and their comparison of the Szczecin and Gdansk shipyards, are both extremely informative.

20. Low wages are not enough to compete on export markets. One of the lessons of a number of case studies is that, even at low wages, goods produced using old technologies often cannot satisfy the quality standards needed to compete in Western export markets.

21. As long as the elasticity of substitution between capital and labour is less than 1, there is a wage low enough that, at that wage, the labour demand shifts down, and a wage high enough that, at that wage, the labour demand shifts up.

22. For a review of the evidence, see Nuti [1996]. For further discussion, and estimation of the degree of undervaluation, see Halpern and Wyplosz [1994].

23. See, for example, Balcerowitz and Gelb [1994]. In the context of China's transition, Brandt and Zhu [1995] develop a model which focuses on the joint evolutions of the private and the state sector, on lending by banks to both sectors, and the implications for money growth and inflation.

24. Inflation was higher than had been forecast. This is relevant, for example, in assessing whether the high nominal interest rates in most countries at the beginning of transition were associated with positive or negative real interest rates. For evidence on forecasts versus realizations for inflation and other variables, see Bruno [1994, table 1-3].

25. Interestingly, the decline in aggregate demand was, I believe, not due primarily to macroeconomic policy. Two important factors were a drop in consumption given income, due perhaps to uncertainty about the future, and a large increase in profit taxes (due to the effect of high inflation on paper profits), leading to an unexpectedly large fiscal surplus.

26. Borensztein *et al.* [1993] present an interesting attempt to decompose the evolution of output in 1991 between 'supply' and 'demand' factors in Romania and Czechoslovakia in 1991. They specify supply in each sector as a function of the relative price, the price of energy and a credit variable. They specify demand in each sector as a function of the relative price, and an aggregate demand component. They attribute roughly two-thirds of the output decline in each of these two countries in 1991 to supply factors, one-third to demand factors. I believe that an extension of this framework to more countries and more years would yield very useful results.

3

Looking at the Pieces

Having looked at the basic mechanisms shaping the transition, I now move back from general to partial equilibrium. I focus on three issues.

I first look at how state firms adjusted to the initial shock of transition. State firms were largely on their own early in the transition, with little supervision or control from the state. This gives us a rare opportunity to learn about the preferences of insiders in firms, unencumbered by the bargaining with outside owners which characterizes wage and employment determination in the West. How did state firms react to the adverse shocks in cost and demand? How did they decide how much to decrease employment and how much to adjust wages? Whose interests were represented? These are some of the questions I take up in the first section of this chapter.

I then turn to the joint issues of restructuring and privatization. To survive, state firms need to do more than adjust to the initial shock. They typically need to change their product lines, to close plants and open new ones, to replace a number of managers, and to replace a good part of their capital equipment. To accelerate the process of restructuring, most Central European countries initially designed ambitious plans for outsider privatization. In most cases—with the important exception of the Czech Republic—strong opposition has led to the demise of those plans. Progress on privatization has been slower than expected, and privatization has more often taken the form of insider than outsider privatization. How much restructuring has actually taken place? Why was there so much opposition to outsider privatization? Does insider privatization make a difference? In the light of what has happened, how should privatization be designed? These are some of the questions I take up in the second section of the chapter. These are central issues for the future: the outcome will determine whether post-communist economies are essentially built de novo, or whether the restructured state firms constitute the core of the manufacturing sector. It will also determine the extent of large-firm closures the government will face in the future, a problem which has proven politically difficult to handle in the West.

The third issue I take up is that of the nature of the labour market in transition. One might have expected that the high degree of reallocation which has characterized transition would lead to a very active labour market. Just the opposite has happened. Large net flows of workers across firms and sectors have been associated with small gross flows. And these flows have largely bypassed the unemployment pool, since many workers have gone directly from one job to another. I examine these facts in the third section of the chapter. Again, these are not only of interest in themselves but also have important implications for the future. A large unemployment pool, and small flows in and out of unemployment, have led to a high proportion of long-term unemployment. One of the lessons of high unemployment in Western Europe is that the long-term unemployed often become marginalized. Will Central Europe be able to avoid the Western European outcome of lingering high unemployment?

I have chosen these three aspects of transition because I have worked on them and I have something to say (even if, as will be painfully clear, I am far from having all the answers). Let me mention two others I would have covered, had I had more space and more knowledge.

The first is credit. Even in the best of cases, transition would have implied the emergence of a credit system where financial intermediaries had no experience in lending, and borrowers had no credit history. But more has been at work. The old relations between state banks and state firms did not disappear overnight, often leading to further accumulation of bad loans. In some cases, clean-ups of existing loans have been followed by the accumulation of new bad loans in anticipation of further clean-ups. In other cases, banks have been allowed to recapitalize through a large wedge between lending and borrowing rates, a solution with low apparent fiscal costs but potentially high costs in terms of growth. The question of how much of the high lending rates can be attributed to equilibrium factors, or to tight money, or to problems within the credit system still needs to be sorted out. The issues are again important, both for the restructuring of state firms and for the development of the new private sector.

The second is the growth of the new private sector. Transition was associated with an explosion of small businesses, often in the trade sector. These businesses required little expertise and little capital. But the evidence on what happened after is more ambiguous. Turnover among new businesses has been very high, a normal phenomenon since competition intensified and many discovered they had chosen the wrong products, or did not have the skills needed to run a business. Evidence on the growth of medium-sized private firms is mixed. This is an important issue, especially if many state firms prove unable to restructure. The nature of the constraints facing these firms (from rent extraction by government officials, to limited access to credit), the nature of the interaction between state (or ex-state) firms and new private firms, and the role of foreign direct investment are the main issues at this point.

3.1 The Initial Adjustment of State Firms

We now have enough evidence, both macro and micro, to have a fairly clear picture of how state firms adjusted to the initial shock of transition. Let me point out what we have learned.[1]

3.1.1 *The hardening of the budget constraint*

As we saw in Chapter 2 (Table 2.1), the start of transition was associated with a dramatic decline in explicit subsidies to state firms. This, however, was just the beginning of the hardening of the budget constraint. Once overt subsidies were gone, state firms explored other avenues. Firms delayed payments of taxes, delayed payments to suppliers, and took bank loans they often did not intend to repay. Such tactics can work only if creditors are willing to oblige. They did initially, in the belief that the government would eventually bail them or their debtors out.[2] Bail-outs indeed came, in some cases, such as Hungary, more than once. But, partly because of the governments' resolve and partly because of the dire fiscal situation, the bail-outs were limited in scope and came with sufficiently many strings attached that, within a few years of transition, most firms came to the conclusion that they now faced a hard budget constraint.[3] The story of how the budget constraint was hardened, of the role of the relative power of the finance ministry, the spending ministries, and the managers of state firms remains to be written. But, today, bad loans are typically concentrated in a small number of firms.[4] The others are operating under something close to a hard budget constraint.

3.1.2 *The appropriation of profits*

Profits were largely appropriated by those working in the firms.

Table 3.1 gives the ratio of accounting profits to sales for the five countries from 1989 to 1992.[5] It makes a simple point. Despite the various wage guidelines in place during most of that period, average accounting profits were driven close to 0.

Table 3.1. Ratio of accounting profits to sales (%)

	1989	1990	1991	1992
Hungary	5.0	3.3	–1.1	—
Poland	28.0	23.3	6.9	3.0
CSFR	9.2	9.4	9.8	—
Czech Republic			(3.0)	(3.0)
Slovak Republic	—	14.4	6.1	0.8
Bulgaria	34.7	14.7	8.2	–2.4

Sources: for all countries except the Czech Republic, data come from Blanchard *et al.* [1995, table 7-5]. The numbers for the Czech Republic come from the appendix to Pohl *et al.* [1996] and are not directly comparable to the others: they are constructed slightly differently (see fn. 5) and cover only the 470 largest Czech firms.

Low or zero profits are no proof of appropriation: profits are low during recessions in the West as well. But the cross-section evidence on the distribution of profits across firms suggests that more was at work than the effect of the output decline. These distributions typically show a bunching of profits at 0. For example, the distribution of profits given by Köllô [1995b] for Hungary in 1991 shows 35 per cent of state firms reporting profit rates between 0 and 5 per cent, 60 per cent of state firms between –5 and 10 per cent. This suggests a deliberate policy on the part of those firms to avoid reporting either accounting profits or losses.

Such appropriation of profits should not come as much of a surprise. Firms were typically put under the formal control of the ministry of finance, away from industrial ministries. The intent was to make clear that the budget constraint was hard.[6] But the ministry of finance had neither the expertise nor the desire to monitor the firms. Thus, in the de facto absence of an owner, why report profits? Why pay profit taxes? Indeed, the relevant question may be why some firms actually reported positive profits. There are probably two reasons. For some firms, wage constraints were binding.[7] And some managers may have wanted to show profits, either as a signal of their abilities, or as a signal of the value of the firm pre-privatization.[8]

3.1.3 The choice of employment and wages

Given the hard budget constraint, and once profits were appropriated, the main decision left to state firms was how much to adjust employment and how much to adjust wages.

To discuss this, it is useful to introduce a simple model. To focus on the interesting part, namely the decision process within the firm, let me make trivial assumptions about technology and demand. Namely, think of a firm as having the following production function:

$$Y \leq N,$$

where N is employment, and Y is output. And assume that the firm takes the level of demand and thus the level of output, Y, as given.

Suppose that output is initially equal to Y_0, with associated level of employment $N_0 = Y_0$, and that transition leads to a reduction in output from Y_0 to $Y_1 < Y_0$. Figure 3.1 plots the average and marginal product after transition. Marginal product is equal to 1 for employment less than $N_1 = Y_1$, equal to 0 thereafter. Average product is equal to 1 for employment less than or equal to N_1, and declines asymptotically to 0 thereafter.

Let w be the market wage (think of it as the wage paid by private firms) and v be the reservation wage, the wage equivalent of being unemployed. I shall endogenize w and v in the next chapter. Here, I take them as given, with $w \geq v$. What employment and wage combination will the state firm choose?

Suppose transfers can be made costlessly between workers, so that those who keep their job can compensate those who lose theirs. Then, without the need for further assumptions,

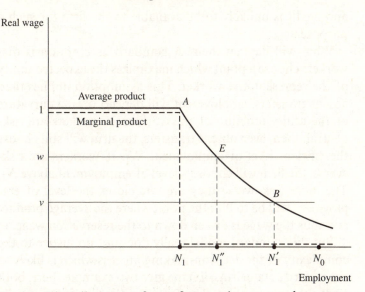

Fig. 3.1. The adjustment of state firm employment and wages to the adverse shift in demand

we know the firm will choose the efficient level of employment, namely $N_1 = Y_1$. This is the level which maximizes total revenues to the initial set of workers, where revenues include the reservation wage times the number of workers laid off by the firm, $(N_0 - N)v$. Absent reasons to report profits, all revenues will then be distributed in some fashion among the initial set of workers, employed or now unemployed. Depending on the decision process, the unemployed may receive a transfer from those who remain employed, and thus receive more than their reservation wage, v.

Transfers from firms to the unemployed are typically limited, even in Western economies. If anything, they are likely to be even more limited in firms in transition. Promises of a steady flow of payments to those laid off by the firm may be difficult to enforce. Severance payments equal to the present value of future payments avoid that problem, but may be difficult for the state firm to pay up-front: the firm is unlikely to have the cash needed to finance them internally, and credit is unlikely to be available to the firm for such a purpose.

What will happen then? A standard assumption is that workers choose a point which maximizes the expected utility of the representative worker. This assumption implies that, absent transfers, employment will depend on the curvature of the utility function of the workers. If workers are risk-neutral, then, even absent transfers, the firm will still choose the efficient level of employment, N_1. If workers are risk-averse, the firm will choose a level of employment above N_1. The more risk-averse they are, the closer the level of employment will be to N_1', the point where the average product and thus the wage is driven down to the reservation wage, v.

But this standard model really does not do justice to the complexity of the decision-making process which is likely to characterize state firms. Let me give two examples here, both under the assumption that there are zero transfers to the unemployed.

(1) Reinterpret the above model as a model of a firm with two plants. Pre-transition, plant 1 employs N_1 workers, plant 2 employs the rest, namely $(N_0 - N_1)$ workers: initial employment in the firm is thus equal to N_0. Suppose that transition eliminates the demand for the output of plant 2. Then, if plant 1 can go its own way, it will; plant 2 will have to close for lack of revenues. Unbundling will lead to the efficient level of employment, N_1.

In this case, the firm will end up at point A. Those N_1 workers who stay employed will earn the average product in plant 1, namely 1. They will be much better off than those who are laid off and earn only the reservation wage, v.[9]

(2) Rather than assuming that workers decide behind a veil of ignorance, assume that for any choice of the level of employment, workers know whether they will be laid off or not. In most cases, this is likely to be a better description of reality than the standard assumption that workers take decisions behind a veil of ignorance: workers with little

seniority, or workers in bad plants, know that they are more at risk than the others. And assume that each worker has veto power. Then the firm will choose employment level N_1', with associated wage v. Any level of employment lower than N_1', and thus associated with an average product above v, will be vetoed by those who lose their jobs. Any level of employment above N_1' would imply that some workers were paid less than their reservation wage; these workers would not want to stay in the firm.

The outcome in this case will be the opposite extreme from that in the previous example. The firm will choose point B. It will maintain the maximum level of employment consistent with the budget constraint, and the wage will be driven down to the reservation wage, v.

With this discussion in mind, we can ask: What wage–employment combination did state firms actually choose? The answer, with all the proper caveats about remaining uncertainties and differences across countries, is that they chose a point close to E in Figure 3.1. Firms which had larger declines in sales had larger declines in relative wages. But, on average, the wage was set substantially above the reservation wage; indeed it was set close to the private wage. And employment was decreased, but not to the point of eliminating labour hoarding. Let me now review the evidence on both wages and employment.

3.1.4 The adjustment of wages

Given the low exit rate from unemployment, we can take the reservation wage for most of the workers who became unemployed as roughly equal to unemployment benefits plus whatever other benefits were provided by the safety net. Maintaining the highest feasible level of employment would have implied driving down the wage in state firms to that level. It is clear that this is not what happened. In all five countries, the average wage in state firms was set at a level roughly equal to the wage in the private sector.[10] In the absence of any evidence of substantial severance payments, it appears that those who were laid off were substantially worse off as a result than those who kept their jobs. One plausible hypothesis is that firms felt that paying a wage roughly equal to the market wage was the only way to avoid crucial workers quitting.[11]

This is not to say that wages were not responsive to specific firm conditions. Firms which had the largest declines in sales also had the largest declines in relative wages. Put another way, the larger the decline in sales, the more willing firms were to cut wages to limit the required decline in employment. Some evidence on the strength of this effect is given in Table 3.2, which summarizes the evidence from a number of firm-level studies for 1990–1 and 1991–2.[12] The coefficients reported in the table are the elasticities of wage changes to sales changes across firms.

I draw two conclusions from the table. First, many of these elasticities are large by standards of Western labour markets (typical coefficients for similar regressions in the United States yield values around 0.05).[13] This is especially true when one takes into account that the estimates in the

Table 3.2. Elasticity of changes in the wage to changes in sales

	1990–1	1991–2
Poland	0.19	
Hungary (1)	0.13*	
Hungary (2)	0.12	
Czech Republic	0.07	0.03
Slovak Republic	0.06	0.13

* 1989–92

Sources: Poland, Czech and Slovak republics, Hungary (2): Estrin and Svejnar [1996].
Hungary (1): Köllô [1996].

table are likely to suffer from a large downward bias due to the poor quality of firm-level data in Central Europe.[14] Second, the table suggests differences across countries. Firms were more willing to cut wages to avoid employment losses in Poland than in the Czech Republic. I shall return to this difference below.

3.1.5 The adjustment of employment

The evolution of employment and the implied evolution of labour productivity were shown in Figures 1.4 and 1.6 in Chapter 1.[15] For the first two to three years of transition, the decrease in output was associated with only a limited decrease in employment, resulting in a sharp drop in productivity. Productivity then recovered, and, except for Bulgaria, now exceeds the pre-transition level.

Who was let go from state firms? The answer is: no group in particular, except for those with clearly higher reservation wages. In Poland, for example, there was a very large increase in early retirements due to the generous eligibility requirements of the pension system. From December 1989 to December 1993, the total number of pensioners increased by 28 per cent, from 6.9 to 8.8 million (Maret and Schwartz 1994). But pre-transition fears that, for example, women might be the first to be laid off were, for the most part, not borne out. The proportion in unemployment has been roughly similar to their proportion in employment. The young have comprised a larger fraction of the unemployed than of the employed. But this is not because they were the first to be laid off, rather because they were not hired. Put another way, at a given rate of unemployment, there do not appear to be clear differences in the composition of unemployment compared to, say, Western Europe.[16]

Going beyond the first few years of transition, should we interpret the fact that labour productivity is now higher than before transition as an indication that employment in state firms is now roughly at the efficient level? The answer is

Table 3.3. Hungary: estimated elasticity of changes in employment to changes in sales

	1986–9	1989–92	1992–3
All firms	0.13	0.33	0.22
Firms with decreasing output	0.21	0.34	0.33
(proportion of firms)	(50%)	(91%)	(66%)
Firms with increasing output	0.01	0.04	0.04
(proportion of firms)	(50%)	(9%)	(34%)

Source: Köllô [1996, table 2]. A constant term is included in the regressions, but is not reported here.

probably no. There was substantial labour hoarding pre-transition, and it is still present. Table 3.3 provides an interesting piece of evidence here. It gives the estimated elasticity of changes in employment to changes in sales based on cross-sections of firms in Hungary in 1986–9, 1989–92, and 1992–3.[17] The elasticities are estimated separately for firms with an increase and firms with a decrease in sales.

The results show a striking asymmetry of the response of employment to sales. While firms which suffered a decrease in output cut employment, firms which experienced an increase in output did not increase employment in response.[18] This suggests that, even by 1992–3, these firms had not eliminated labour hoarding, and were therefore able to satisfy the increase in production with their existing workers. Anticipating the discussion of restructuring in the next section, this also suggests that much of the increase in labour productivity since 1992 has come from this mechanism rather than from deeper restructuring measures; more on this below.

3.1.6 *The role of labour market conditions*

I have focused so far on insider effects, on the reaction of wages (and the implied adjustment of employment) to firm-specific factors. Another dimension is how wages responded to labour market conditions. The time-series are too short, and too many factors are at work, to hope to learn anything from time-series relation between unemployment and wages. But one can learn something from the cross-regional evidence.

Figure 3.2 (taken from the EU *Employment Observatory*, May 1995) shows the map of unemployment in 1995 in Central Europe. It shows how the very different industrial structures, coupled with low labour mobility, have led to very different unemployment rates across regions.[19] This heterogeneity offers a potentially clear test of the effects of unemployment on wages, along the lines of Blanchflower and Oswald [1994]. Given that unemployment rates were close to 0 in all regions pre-transition, the effects of unemployment can be separated from region fixed effects. And the evidence points to a growing and significant effect of unemployment.[20] For example, using individual wage data, firm and worker controls, and regional unemployment rates, Köllô [1996] finds, for Hungary, an elasticity of the wage to the unemployment rate of −0.05 in 1989, −0.10 in 1992, and −0.12 in 1993. By way of comparison, this last number is slightly higher than that estimated by Blanchflower and Oswald for the United States using a similar specification.

3.1.7 Tentative conclusions

In the end, the main features of the initial adjustment of state firms are perhaps not surprising. Once the budget constraint was hardened, firms had to trade off employment against wages. Firms with the largest adverse shocks accepted the largest relative wage declines. But firms could not decrease the wage too much, for fear of losing their essential workers to the private sector. Employment was reduced but not to the core, leaving firms with excess employment.

I have focused so far on the common features of the

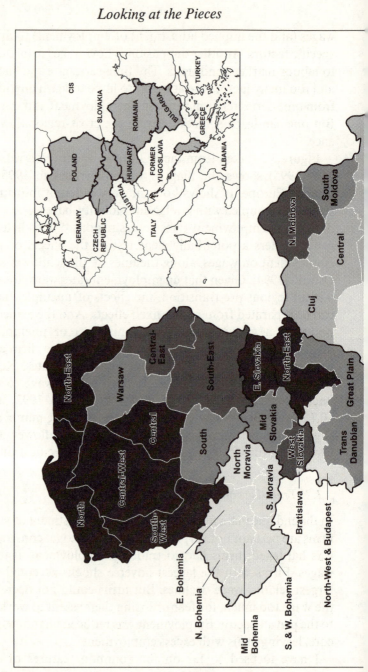

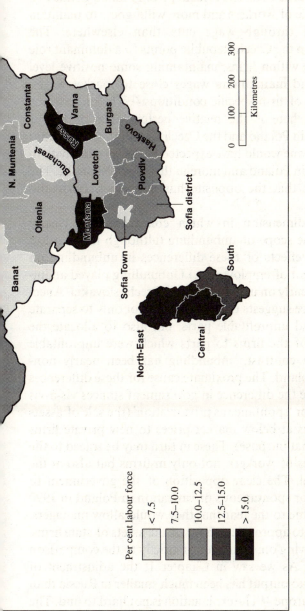

Fig. 3.2. Regional unemployment, 1995(2)

adjustment across countries. The numbers suggest important differences as well. The evidence from Poland points to a dominant role of workers and more willingness to maintain employment through wage cuts than elsewhere. The evidence from the Czech Republic points to a dominant role of managers within firms, maintaining some positive level of profits and maintaining wages close to market wages, independent of firm-specific conditions.[21] The piece which does not fit here is the relative performance of labour productivity in Poland and the Czech Republic. Other things being equal, one would have expected labour productivity to increase less in Poland and more in the Czech Republic. The data suggest that the opposite has happened. I have no resolution.

Another dimension in which countries have clearly differed is the scope of unbundling (although it is hard to identify any effects of these differences in unbundling on the adjustment of employment.) Unbundling played an important role early on in Hungary and Czechoslovakia. Anecdotal evidence suggests that it was used not only to separate profitable and unprofitable parts, but also to allocate the initial debt of the firms to parts which were unprofitable anyway.[22] In contrast, unbundling has been nearly nonexistent in Poland. The proximate cause for these differences appears to be the difference in government stances vis-à-vis unbundling or 'spontaneous privatization' (the sale of assets by state firms at below market prices to new private firms created for that purpose). These in turn may be traced to the different roles of workers, not only in firms but also at the political level. The clear opposition of the government to unbundling or spontaneous privatization in Poland in 1990 was largely due to the fear that they would allow managers, not workers, to appropriate many of the assets of state firms.

Before moving on, let me return briefly to the comparison with Russia. As we saw in Chapter 1, the adjustment of employment to output has been much smaller in Russia than in Central Europe.[23] The explanation is not hard to find. The reservation wage in Russia has been very low: losing a job means not only receiving low unemployment benefits, but often also losing many benefits which have traditionally been supplied within the firm. Not surprisingly, this has led firms to choose relatively less employment adjustment and more wage adjustment than in Central Europe. Interestingly, and in contrast with Central Europe, something like an explicit two-tier wage structure has emerged: some workers receive no or very low wages but keep their access to the benefits offered by the firm.

3.2 Restructuring and Privatization

The initial adjustment of firms has sometimes been taken as evidence of restructuring by state firms. But the word 're-structuring' is misleading in this context. What firms did was to take the measures needed to meet their hardening budget constraint. Using the terminology introduced by Grosfeld and Roland [1994], the initial adjustment reflected *defensive restructuring*. What state firms need to do to survive and grow is *strategic restructuring*.

3.2.1 The two dimensions of restructuring

I shall review some of the quantitative evidence on restructuring later in the section. At this stage, let me just state that I read the bulk of the evidence as saying that state firms (and here I mean state firms *pre-privatization*) have not engaged in extensive deep restructuring.[24]

This finding should come as no surprise. Deep restructuring (which I shall call simply 'restructuring' from now on) has two relevant dimensions here.

(1) First, even if it does not require further decreases in employment, it surely implies that some of those currently

employed will lose their job. Many of the existing managers do not have the right skills and must be replaced. Some of the existing operations or plants have to be closed; even if new ones are created, not all of the original employees are likely to be kept on.

All the issues we discussed in Section 3.1 are relevant here. Unless they can be compensated, those whose jobs are at risk will oppose such changes. Managers who know that they do not have the right skills will oppose them. So will workers in plants which are likely to be closed. For the same reasons as before, the outcome is likely to be a strong bias in favour of the status quo.

(2) Second, restructuring is likely to require large capital expenditures. The capital equipment of state firms is typically old and technologically obsolete. The proportion of equipment in industry less than 5 years old was estimated in the early 1990s to be around 19 per cent in Poland, 23 per cent in Czechoslovakia, 29 per cent in Hungary, compared to 40 per cent in Germany.[25] Restructuring typically implies replacing much of this equipment.

State firms are unlikely to have the funds to finance such outlays. Financing them from retained earnings may be difficult, and is unappealing in the absence of well-defined rights to future profits. The same property rights issues are likely to rule out equity finance (unless the firm is privatized in the process, the issue to which I shall turn next), or large debt finance.

Thus, for both sets of reasons, state firms are unlikely to restructure. It is useful to introduce a simple formalization at this point. It will not do much for now, but will help clarify the discussion below.

Take a state firm after the initial adjustment. Assume that employment is equal to N, and the wage is equal to the average product of labour, x. Let, as before, w and v denote the market and the reservation wage respectively. Given the evidence in the previous section, let me assume that $x \geq w > v$.

Formalize restructuring as follows. First, restructuring requires that only a proportion λ of workers stay in the firm. The others must be replaced. The assumption that total employment in the firm does not change is both for convenience and to make it obvious that the type of restructuring we are looking at here—which keeps employment constant and increases the average product of workers—is socially desirable. Second, restructuring requires the addition of new capital. If both conditions are met, the average product net of the user cost of new capital per worker increases from x to $x(1 + \theta)$, where $\theta > 0$.

Thus, restructuring leaves total employment in the firm unchanged and increases the average product. Will restructuring take place? Not if the workers who are at risk from restructuring can oppose it and cannot be bribed out of their opposition: if fired, they stand to lose $(x - v)$. And not if the firm cannot get the funds to buy the new capital. Let me now turn to the scope and the role of privatization in this context.

3.2.2 *The opposition to outsider privatization*

The fact that state firms were unlikely to restructure was the motivation behind the initial programmes for large-scale outsider privatization. Outsiders would, it was argued, have both the incentives and the ability to restructure. They could raise the capital, and could ignore or appease the opposition from those who were likely to lose out from restructuring.

Two approaches were taken. One included the traditional methods of privatization used in the West, from direct sales to auctions to potential outside investors. The other was mass privatization. But, as transition proceeded—and with the exception of the Czech Republic—mass-privatization plans were either shelved or drastically reduced in scope. And direct sales to outsiders were few in number.

The problem turned out to be the opposition of insiders in firms. They were opposed to privatization for the same reasons that they were opposed to restructuring. While they

typically received some shares for free under mass privatization, their stakes in the privatized firm were small. Thus, they
perceived privatization and subsequent restructuring as
putting their jobs at risk and implying a potential wage cut
for those who remained employed. The fears that outsider
privatization triggered are clear from a survey of 1,500
employees of state-owned companies in Poland in 1993.
These workers were asked: 'If the company in which you are
employed becomes privatized, what do you think the private
owner will do? Choose 3 answers.' The tabulation of their
answers is given in Table 3.4.

Table 3.4. Privatization fears and hopes

Fire all unneeded workers	76%
Squeeze the company for profit for a short time	44%
Employ competent workers in all positions	38%
Replace some of the executives in the company	29%
Buy new equipment and machines	23%
Limit the role of employees in decisions	21%
Limit the role of unions	19%
Increase wages	18%
Improve working conditions	8%

Source: Centrum Badania Opinii Spolecznej [1993].

Given their opposition, workers and managers were often
able to ensure that their firm was neither sold to outsiders
nor put on the mass-privatization list. At the national level,
they were able to delay, often indefinitely, mass-privatization
programmes. The single exception is the Czech Republic.
Why was it successful in implementing its programme? Two
explanations are typically given. The first is that, because of
tighter control of firms pre-transition, managers of firms
were less powerful vis-à-vis the government than in the other
countries, and thus less able to block privatization. The
second is that the period of 'extraordinary politics' and
public support immediately following transition was used

more effectively in the Czech Republic to start a privatization process which, once it had started, was harder to stop (although not impossible, as the suspension of mass privatization in the Slovak Republic made clear in 1995). In contrast, the complex design of the Polish mass-privatization plan, especially the need to set up state-appointed investment funds, implied delays and more time to block privatization.

The lessons of these early failures were incorporated into the design of Russian privatization. The conclusion was that, given that in Russia the period of extraordinary politics had already come and gone, the only way to achieve large-scale privatization was to enlist the support of the insiders in firms (and buy off whatever other constituencies there were whose support was needed for the implementation of privatization, such as local authorities), and thus to give insiders a large stake in the privatized firms.[26] The result was mass insider privatization. In most privatized Russian firms, insiders have either a large minority or a majority stake in the firm. Central European countries have been reluctant to follow the Russian route. But there as well, the privatization that has taken place has mostly taken the form of insider privatization. And the current 'mass-privatization' programmes (which are often all but mass in size) typically give a larger stake to insiders than earlier ones.

This raises a simple question. Does insider privatization lead to restructuring? Note that there are in fact two different questions here. The first is: Does insider *ownership* lead to restructuring? The second is: If it does not, will it lead to resale to outsiders who will then restructure? Let me take both questions in turn.

3.2.3 *Insider ownership and restructuring*

Let me start with the first of the two questions. Let me consider pure insider ownership, the case where the firm is given or sold at a discount to the insiders in the firm, managers and workers. The conclusions extend straightforwardly to the more realistic case where privatization leads only to majority insider ownership.

From the earlier discussion of restructuring in state firms, it is clear that insider ownership will alleviate but not eliminate the obstacles to restructuring facing state firms pre-privatization.

Take the need for new capital. With well-established property rights, insiders will now have an incentive to generate profits and use retained earnings to buy new equipment. But retained earnings are likely to be insufficient, and outside finance may still be limited. Equity financing is likely to be unavailable. Nobody will want to provide equity if the majority shareholders, here the workers, can appropriate future profits through payment of higher wages (an issue faced by employee-owned firms in the West as well). Debt finance may now be available but, again, as in the West, there are limits to the degree of leverage firms will want to accept in order to buy new capital.[27]

Take the issues of job loss and opposition to restructuring by those who will lose their jobs. They will now have less to lose, since what they lose as workers may be partly offset by what they gain as shareholders (although, again, they may suffer from being outside minority shareholders: if future profits are paid in the form of higher wages to then current workers, they may not have access to future profits). Also the firm, having more access to external finance, may have more ability to pay larger severance payments. But this may not be enough.

Thus, how much restructuring can be carried out under insider ownership is ultimately an empirical question. An obvious first step in trying to answer this question is to look at the relative performance of firms under different ownership structures. The results of a number of studies, in particular of studies carried out by the World Bank based on surveys of firms, are summarized in EBRD [1995, ch. 8]. Some of the findings from surveys of firms in Hungary and Poland in 1993 are reproduced in Table 3.5.[28]

If we take the proportion of firms introducing new tech-

Table 3.5. Performance of firms in Hungary and Poland, by ownership type, 1993

	Ownership			
	State	Insiders	Outsiders	
			Domestic	Foreign
Hungary				
Employees per firm	699	293	74	364
% new technologies	13.9	16.7	23.1	42.9
Investment-to-sales ratio (%)	0.6	0.2*	1.1*	1.1*
Poland				
Employees per firm	548	273	132	432
% new technologies	51.6	75.0	71.4	87.5
Investment-to-sales ratio (%)	1.2	2.8*	0.0*	5.8*

* computed on the basis of ten firms or fewer

Note: '% new technologies' is the percentage of firms reporting major investment in new technology within the previous two years.

Source: EBRD [1995, ch. 8, table 8-5].

nologies as a rough index of restructuring, the evidence from both countries suggests a ranking with state firms at the bottom, insider-owned firms next, domestic-outsider-owned next, and finally foreign-outsider-owned firms at the top. (The differences in levels between Hungary and Poland are striking; but I suspect that they must partly reflect differences in the definition of what a new technology is.) The numbers on investment-to-sales ratios suggest a roughly similar ranking, but with a few surprises, perhaps due to small sample sizes. To put the investment-to-sales ratio numbers in perspective, recall the investment-to-sales ratio in manufacturing in the United States is around 6 per cent: the numbers in the table are low by comparison.

The problem in interpreting Table 3.5 is whether the

Table 3.6. Russian firms: actions, decisions, and perceptions, by ownership type

	State	Privatized	New private
Restructuring:			
% investing in new equipment	33.7	45.0	46.7
% changing product lines	35.3	48.9	44.8
% with incentive pay	29.6	41.2	65.2
Decision-making influence:			
Ministry	37.7	24.9	8.7
Managers	67.1	72.5	47.8
Workers	21.9	25.4	2.3
Customers	52.7	63.7	80.9

Note: Each number gives the percentage of workers answering yes to the corresponding question.

Source: Earle and Rose [1996, tables 2, 3, and 5].

correlations between ownership status and restructuring can be interpreted as causal. Do, for example, foreign-owned firms do better because they are owned by foreigners, or because they were better to start with, attracting the attention of foreigners in the first place? The right approach would be to exploit differences in privatization rules across regions or countries; I have not seen this done yet. A much cruder approach is to look at Russia in recent years. Which firms were already privatized and which firms were still in state hands in, say, 1995 was more likely to depend on relative speeds of privatization in one region or another than on the choice of firms to be privatized or not. With that motivation, let me present in Table 3.6 the results from a 1995 survey by Earle and Rose [1996] asking workers questions about the status of their firm—state, privatized (most likely insider privatized, but the question was not asked), and private de novo—and their perceptions of the decision-making process within the firm. The table gives a fairly clear picture, one of insider-owned firms doing more restructuring than state firms but less than new private firms; of insider-owned firms being less dependent on ministries than state firms but less tuned to the market than new private firms.

If insider ownership goes only some of the way, as both theory and the empirical evidence suggests, the question of resale becomes essential. Let me now turn to that.

3.2.4 *Insider ownership and resale*

If insiders cannot restructure, won't they at least have the incentive to sell to those who can? The answer is: not necessarily. To see why, let me return to the example I introduced earlier.[29]

Assume that decisions are taken behind a veil of ignorance: workers have equal probability $(1 - \lambda)$ of losing their job under restructuring, so that all workers are ex ante identical. And assume that each worker has one share of the firm.

Let me start with the case where workers do not coordinate: each worker decides or not to sell his share, taking the decisions of other workers as given. Let q be the price of a share. Conditional on getting enough shares to be able to restructure, the maximum price a buyer will be willing to pay for a share is given by

$$q^b = x(1 + \theta) - w. \tag{2.1}$$

The maximum buying price is equal to the average product per worker post-restructuring minus the market wage. Turn now to the selling price. Conditional on enough shares being sold so that restructuring will take place, the minimum price a worker will be willing to sell his share for is defined by

$$q^s + \lambda w + (1 - \lambda)v = (x(1 + \theta) - w) + \lambda w + (1 - \lambda)v. \tag{2.2}$$

Whether or not he sells his own share, the worker takes as given that the firm will be restructured, so that with probability λ he will remain employed in the firm at market wage w, and with probability $(1 - \lambda)$ he will become unemployed and receive his reservation wage, v. If he sells, he will receive price q^s; if he does not, he will remain a shareholder in the new firm and thus receive dividends $(x(1 + \theta) - w)$. Equations (2.1) and (2.2) imply that

$$q^s = q^b = x(1 + \theta) - w.$$

Thus, the selling and the buying price are the same: resale will take place. This result is familiar from the work of Grossman and Hart [1980]: dispersed shareholders (in this case worker–owners) will bid the price up until they extract all the surplus from restructuring by the next owner; but the sale will go through. Indeed, based on the experience of Russia, and going beyond the assumptions of this example, one can think of a number of reasons why in fact workers will be willing to sell shares at a price substantially lower than q^b, removing the razor edge nature of the result above. To the extent that dividends will accrue only in the future, workers may value current cash (relative to future cash) more than the buyer does, and thus be willing to accept less than the present value, q^b. Or, workers may expect the new owner to dilute their ownership claim to future dividends, and thus may expect to receive only a fraction of $(x(1 + \theta) - w)$ in the future if they remain shareholders; in this case again, they will be willing to settle for less than q^b. The evidence from Russia is that, for these or other reasons, workers were indeed often willing to sell their share at a fraction of its fundamental value.

Things are quite different when the decision to resell is taken collectively by workers. In that case, the maximum price a buyer will be willing to pay for a share is still given by equation (2.1). But the minimum price at which workers collectively will be willing to sell is now defined by

$$q^s + \lambda w + (1 - \lambda)v = x. \tag{2.3}$$

The left-hand side shows what the workers get in expected value if they sell and the firm is restructured, namely the price of the share, plus the market wage if they are retained by the firm, and the reservation wage if they are not. The right-hand side gives what they will get if they collectively decide not to sell, namely the average product absent restructuring. The sale will take place if $q^s \leq q^b$, or equivalently, using equations (2.1) and (2.3):

$$x\theta \geq (1 - \lambda)(w - v).$$

The left-hand side is the increase in the average product under restructuring. The right-hand side is the expected loss to the workers coming from the risk of unemployment. Thus, if they act collectively, workers will not necessarily agree to resale. The higher the probability of being laid off, or the larger the difference between the market wage and the reservation wage, the more opposition there will be to resale.[30]

Let me draw the main conclusions from this and the previous subsection. The evidence is that outside ownership is typically needed for full restructuring to take place. It is also clear that political constraints often require insider privatization, or at least generous terms to the insiders. Fortunately, these two requirements are not incompatible. Insider privatization can be designed in such a way that, if insider ownership does not lead to restructuring, it will lead to resale, and thus to eventual outsider ownership and privatization. But, to make sure that this happens, it is important to design privatization to prevent collusion in resale. This has a number of practical implications.

It is important for example that some shares be given or sold to outsiders, so that there is a market for shares where workers can sell their shares anonymously. It is important that shares not be registered at the firm, so that workers can sell their shares without threats of reprisal by other workers or managers. It is important that shares not be put in funds under the control of managers, who can then more easily organize collusion, and so on.[31] Should, from the point of view of resale, the state give relatively more shares to managers (and less to workers)? The answer is ambiguous. On the one hand, the presence of large shareholders (the managers) makes it easier for collusion to block resale. On the other hand, to the extent that managers can convince outside buyers to keep them on, they will be more aggressive in finding such buyers and realizing the sale. There is anec-dotal evidence that both effects have been at work in Russia. In a number of cases, managers have convinced foreign investors both to buy the firm and to keep them on, probably leading to faster restructuring of the firm.

3.3 Reallocation, Flows, and Unemployment

Given the size of the reallocation process at work in Central Europe, one might have expected the emergence of a very active labour market, with large flows in and out of unemployment. This has not been the case. In most countries, unemployment has been a stagnant pool, and the proportion of long-term unemployed has steadily increased. It is important to understand why.

3.3.1 Net and gross flows

It is not that reallocation has not taken place. I gave in Chapter 1 measures of the degree of reallocation (the stand-ard deviation of employment changes across sectors) in the various countries and showed that these were indeed very high by OECD standards. Restructuring may not be pro-ceeding very rapidly, but reallocation is. Some sectors are de-clining, others increasing; the ex-state sector is contracting, the new private sector is expanding.

High net flows between firms or sectors do not necessarily imply high gross flows of workers, however. It is well known that, in labour markets in the West, quits are procyclical: in a recession, as more workers lose their jobs and labour market conditions worsen, others are more reluctant to quit, mitigating the effects of larger lay-offs on total worker flows. This effect has been very much at work in Central Europe as well. This is clearly shown in Table 3.7, taken from Konings

Table 3.7. Gross job and worker flows: Polish state enterprises in manufacturing, 1989–1991

	Job destruction	Job creation	Separations	Hirings
1989	0.061	0.020	0.229	0.179
1990	0.153	0.006	0.276	0.129
1991	0.176	0.010	0.260	0.097
United States	0.102	0.091	0.515	0.506

Note: US values for separations and hirings in manufacturing are means for the period 1951–1981 (the series were discontinued in 1981).

Source: Konings *et al.* [1995]; US values for job destruction and job creation are taken from Davis *et al.* [1996].

et al. [1995], which shows the evolution of job and worker flows in Poland from 1989 to 1991.

The first two columns give 'job flows'. Following Davis *et al.* [1996], 'job destruction' is equal to the sum of employment changes in all firms which had a decrease in employment during the year, divided by total average employment during the year. 'Job creation' is equal to the sum of employment changes in all firms which had an increase in employment during the year, divided again by total employment. The next two columns give 'worker flows', namely total separations and hirings for the same set of firms. For comparison, the last line gives corresponding US manufacturing numbers (averages for 1951–81).[32]

The first two columns paint a now familiar story. Early transition in Poland was associated with a sharp increase in job destruction and a drop in job creation. But, the third column shows, this sharp increase in job destruction was not reflected in a parallel increase in separations. This is the effect I mentioned earlier. The large lay-offs triggered by transition were largely offset by a drop in quits, leading to only a small increase in total separations. On the hiring side, the result of lower job creation and lower quits (and thus fewer workers to replace) was a dramatic decrease in hirings. In short, early transition in Poland was characterized by a large increase in net flows, but not much change in gross flows, which remained much lower than in the United States. The scattered evidence suggests that gross flows have remained low in most countries since then.[33]

An interesting side question here is why, given their desire to decrease employment, state firms in Poland were hiring at all in 1990 and 1991: the hiring rate was around 10 per cent in both years. Heterogeneity is clearly part of the answer: some firms had an increase in employment. But the main reason, I suspect, is that, even in firms which wanted to decrease overall employment, some of the workers who quit had to be replaced. A hint of the importance of this effect and the Leontief nature of the technology—more precisely, the imperfect substitutability between workers in the firm— is given in Köllô [1995a]: in Hungary, firms which had a decline in orders still replaced 14 per cent of their unskilled workers in 1992, 21 per cent in 1994. For skilled manual workers, the two numbers were 26 per cent and 31 per cent respectively.

3.3.2 *Flows between employment, unemployment, and non-participation*

Figures 3.3 and 3.4, taken from Blanchard *et al.* [1995], give the flows of workers between private employment, state employment, unemployment, and non-participation in Poland and in Hungary in 1992. These figures, which patch together information from LFS surveys and data on firms, provide a number of insights into the workings of the labour markets in the two countries. The numbers in the figures give the size of the flows and the stocks, expressed in millions of workers.

The aspect I want to focus on here is the high proportion of hirings directly from employment, rather than from either unemployment or non-participation. In 1992 in Poland, 40

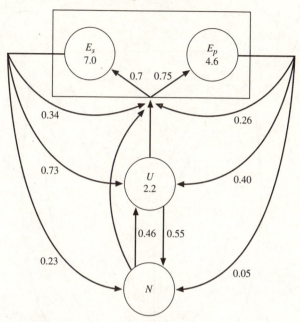

Fig. 3.3. Labour market flows, Poland, 1992

per cent of those hired by firms came directly from employment, compared to 45 per cent from unemployment and
15 per cent from non-participation. In Hungary, the
corresponding proportions were 71 per cent, 12 per cent, and
17 per cent respectively. Compare this to 20 per cent, 37 per
cent, and 43 per cent respectively in the United States.[34] Why
was the proportion of hirings from employment relatively so
high? I believe the main reason is the poor initial matching of
workers and firms. In an economy which has been a market
economy for a long time, most workers have tried a number
of jobs and are happy in their current job; they are thus not
actively looking for work. This is not true of transition
economies. There, many of those employed in state firms
were in effect randomly matched; a larger proportion of them
are likely to be looking for jobs. This is why the proportion of
hirings from employment has been higher than in the West.[35]

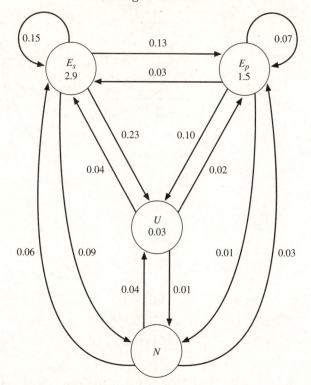

Fig. 3.4. Labour market flows, Hungary, 1992

3.3.3 The plight of the unemployed

Low overall levels of hiring, and competition with those still employed in the state sector, have combined to make it difficult for the unemployed to find jobs. In Chapter 1, I plotted both the total exit rate from unemployment and the exit rate from unemployment to employment for Poland since 1992, and showed how low these were in comparison to labour markets in the West. The first two columns of Table 3.8 give the mean value of the same two monthly exit rates for the five countries in 1994.

With the exception of the Czech Republic, the exit rate from unemployment has been very low. And the exit rate

Table 3.8. Unemployment: exit rates, duration, and coverage (%)

	Exit rate (total)	Exit rate to employment	Proportion long-term unemployed	Proportion receiving benefits
Poland	6.1	3.1	40	50
Hungary	17.5	4.9	48	43
Czech Republic	20.3	15.3	31	52
Slovak Republic	7.4	2.0	53	22
Bulgaria	8.4	1.2	65	36
United States	36.0	24.0	9	

Source: Columns 1 and 2, for 1994, come from Boeri [1995]; columns 3 and 4, for 1995(2), come from the Employment Observatory: Central and Eastern Europe.

from unemployment to employment has been even lower.[36] The result of these low exit rates has been a steady increase in the proportion of long-term unemployment. As shown in the third column of Table 3.8, in the second quarter of 1995, the proportion of unemployed who had been unemployed for more than a year was close to, or above, 50 per cent for three of the five countries.

At the same time, unemployment benefits have become less generous than at the start of transition.[37] Benefit rates are between 50 and 65 per cent of previous wage (in Poland, 36 per cent of the economy-wide average wage). The duration of benefits is typically twelve months or less. The combination of limited duration of benefits and long actual duration of unemployment has led to a steady decline in the proportion of the unemployed who receive unemployment benefits.

In short, the unemployment pool has been stagnant. Unemployment benefits have not been particularly generous. Returning to the theme of the previous section, it is not difficult to understand why workers have generally opposed measures which put their jobs at risk, such as privatization or restructuring.

NOTES

1. Much of what I know here comes from participating in two World Bank studies on this topic. The first study was based on aggregate and sectoral data; the results are reported in Commander and Coricelli [1995]. Blanchard *et al.* [1995] provides an overview of the results. The second, which is still on-going, has looked at the evidence from large panels of state firms. I rely in particular below on Estrin and Svejnar [1996]; Commander and Dhar [1996] on Poland; and Köllô [1996] on Hungary.

2. For more on the dynamics of arrears and bank loans, see, for example, Belka *et al.* [1995] on Poland; Bonin and Schaffer

[1995] on Hungary. For a look at Russia, and how the dynamics of hardening differ from those in Central Europe, see Alfandari and Schaffer [1996].

3. For more on Poland, see Blanchard *et al.* [1993, ch. 4].

4. For evidence on the distribution of bad loans among Polish firms, see Gomulka [1994].

5. The exact definition of profits varies from country to country. In general, profits are equal to revenues from sales minus labour and materials costs (at historical cost), minus depreciation (also at historical cost) and interest payments. The numbers constructed by Pohl *et al.* [1996] for the Czech firms differ in that profits are adjusted for depreciation at replacement cost. As measures of economic profit, these measures suffer from a number of serious problems. For example, the very high accounting profits in Poland in 1990 were in fact paper profits, due to the valuation of materials at historical costs during a period of high inflation (see Schaffer 1992 for further discussion). But my purpose here is precisely to look at what happened to accounting, not economic profits.

6. The experience of Russia (where this was not done) suggests that separating state firms from their ministries was indeed a wise move, at least in terms of hardening the budget constraint.

7. See the 'country papers' in Commander and Coricelli [1995].

8. For further discussion of the role and objectives of managers in state firms, see, for example, Aghion *et al.* [1994]; Commander and McHale [1996].

9. Unilateral unbundling may be illegal or costly. What happens then will depend on the costs that plant 2 can inflict on plant 1, and thus on the organizational structure of the state firm. For further discussion of the role and scope of unbundling, and a number of examples, see Aghion *et al.* [1994].

10. See for example the numbers in Blanchard *et al.* [1995, table 7-6]. The statement holds with a number of qualifications. In particular, non-wage benefits have typically been higher in state firms. Wages in foreign-owned private firms have typically been higher than in other private firms, and thus higher than in state firms.

11. This raises the question of why firms did not pay different wages depending both on the value of the workers to the firm

and on their outside opportunities. The answer may be found in the same factors I emphasized when discussing disorganization in Chapter 2, such as the difficulty for the firm of assessing the value of outside opportunities. Interestingly, as we shall see below, something like a two-tier system has been adopted by firms in Russia.

12. The table comes with two main caveats. First, each number in the table is obtained by combining the estimated elasticities from two different regressions, the elasticity of changes in employment to changes in output, and the elasticity of the change of the wage to changes in labour productivity. A regression of the change in the wage on the change in sales would not in general yield exactly the same results (the results from such a regression were not available). Second, the specification of the underlying regressions, such as the set of controls included in the regression, varies from country to country.

13. See, for example, Freeman and Katz [1991].

14. Some indication of the importance of the bias comes from the results of Commander and Dhar [1996], who use Polish data aggregated by 2-digit/region cell. They obtain elasticities of 0.38 for 1990–1 and 0.42 for 1991–2, thus about twice the values from firm-level elasticities reported in the table. (They obtain elasticities of 0.17 for 1992–3, and 0.25 for 1993–4, suggesting a decline in elasticities as transition went on.)

15. The new private manufacturing sector played a sufficiently small role in the first few years of transition that the figures can be interpreted as giving the behaviour of employment and productivity in state firms.

16. See, for example, the comparison to Spain and France in Blanchard *et al.* [1995, fig. 7-6].

17. The reason for including the first subperiod, 1986 to 1989, is that Hungarian firms were given substantially more autonomy from the mid-1980s on.

18. Results from Poland in Commander and Dhar [1996], using data by sector–region cells suggest a similar pattern, at least early in transition. Interestingly, the asymmetry disappears from 1992 on.

19. In 1994, the rate of interregional migration in Poland was 0.42 per cent, compared to a range of 1 to 2.5 per cent across Western European countries (Bentolila 1997).

20. See, for example, Boeri and Scarpetta [1994] for cross-regional evidence in the Czech and the Slovak republics, Poland, and Hungary.
21. Another factor was probably that wage guidelines were more binding in the Czech Republic. (I have not seen a study assessing the relative importance of managers compared to guidelines.)
22. See, for example, Lizal *et al.* [1995] for evidence for the Czech Republic.
23. Put another way, Russian firms have adjusted hours per worker relatively more, the number of workers relatively less. For a description of the adjustment of state firms in Russia along lines parallel to those of this section, see Commander *et al.* [1996]. See also Layard and Richter [1995].
24. See, for example, the surveys by Carlin *et al.* [1994] and Grosfeld and Roland [1994], and EBRD [1995, ch. 8].
25. This number comes from OECD [1992, table 6].
26. The logic of the Russian privatization programme is beautifully articulated in Boycko *et al.* [1995].
27. The problem of debt finance is exacerbated when, as has been the case in one of the insider-privatization options open to firms in Poland, firms are bought from the state through a long-term lease, creating high leverage from the start.
28. Two of the numbers in the table for Poland in the EBRD report were typos. They are corrected here. I am indebted to Mark Schaffer for pointing them out to me.
29. A more thorough discussion of the issues in this section is given in Aghion and Blanchard [1996].
30. Note that this turns one of the results of Shleifer and Vishny [1986] on its head. Shleifer and Vishny argued that the presence of large shareholders made takoever bids more likely. Here, the effect is ambiguous. The Shleifer–Vishny result obtains if $w = v$. In that case, workers will proceed with resale as long as $x\theta$, the rents from restructuring, are positive. The additional effect, which makes the outcome ambiguous, is the presence of a wedge between the market wage and the reservation wage. Each worker hired from unemployment costs the firm w, but each existing worker becoming unemployed receives v. This result is closely related to the discussion in corporate finance of how, if managers enjoy benefits of control, they may block

an efficient sale. The wedge here is not the benefits of control for managers, but rather the difference between the wage and the reservation wage for workers.

31. See Frydman *et al.* [1995] for some evidence from Russia.

32. In comparing the United States and Poland, one should keep in mind that the average manufacturing firm employs 400 workers in Poland, compared to 70 in the United States. Smaller firms typically have larger turnover.

33. Boeri [1996] examines available numbers for a number of Central European countries.

34. These estimates come from Blanchard and Diamond [1990].

35. Shimer [1995] has constructed a model of transition which is based exactly on this mechanism. He formalizes transition as a process where, starting from random matching, workers and firms try matches until they have found the right one. His model is one of efficient reorganization: transition leads to a period of unemployment, and steadily increasing productivity.

36. As a matter of arithmetic, most of the difference between these exit rates from unemployment to employment across countries comes from the difference in unemployment rates rather than from the difference in the size of the flows. The exit rate from unemployment to employment is defined as $(FUN)/U$, where FUN is the flow from unemployment to employment in a given month. Rewrite it as $(FUN)/(N + U)$, the flow from unemployment to employment normalized by the labour force, times $U/(N + U)$, the unemployment rate. The first term (the normalized flow) varies from 0.62% per month in the Czech Republic to 0.25% in Bulgaria, a ratio of about 2.5, compared to a ratio of more than 10 for the exit rates.

37. Details about unemployment benefit levels and rules are given in the *Employment Observatory, Central and Eastern Europe*, no. 7, May 1995.

4

Putting the Pieces Together

In Chapter 1, I focused on the U-shaped adjustment of output and unemployment during transition. In Chapter 2, I argued that the two main forces shaping transition were reallocation—from old to new activities, from state firms to new private firms—and restructuring—of existing state firms. In Chapter 3, I looked in particular at the interaction between restructuring and labour market conditions. In this last chapter, I want to put these elements together in a small, general equilibrium, model of transition.

I start by building a benchmark version of the model in Section 4.1. The focus is on the interaction between growth of the new private sector, restructuring of firms in the state sector, and unemployment. Private sector growth decreases unemployment. Restructuring of state firms increases output but increases unemployment. Unemployment in turn affects both private sector growth and the speed of restructuring. In the benchmark model, these effects combine to give two phases of transition. In the first, high unemployment prevents restructuring, and the action only comes from private sector growth. In the second, the economy proceeds along a balanced path, where private sector employment creation absorbs the employment losses from restructuring. Output grows as a result of both reallocation and restructuring, and unemployment remains constant until transition has been achieved. The picture of transition drawn by the model is stark, but strikes me as the right one: worse initial shocks lead to higher unemployment, slow down restructuring, and delay the transition. Private sector employment growth not only increases employment directly, but also facilitates re-structuring and transition.

One of the motivations for building a general equilibrium model is to assess the full effects of alternative policies. In Section 4.2, I look at two policies. The first is unemployment insurance. The main motivation for introducing unemployment benefits is clearly distributional. But the question has arisen of whether unemployment benefits may also be justi-fied on efficiency grounds, whether they may facilitate trans-ition by making restructuring less unappealing to workers in state firms. The answer from the model is ambiguous: more generous unemployment benefits may or may not lead to an earlier start to restructuring. This depends on their effects on restructuring decisions on the one hand, and on wages and thus private sector growth on the other. The second policy is privatization. Here, the model largely confirms the partial equilibrium results of Chapter 3. Well-designed privatiza-tion rules, which give more to insiders and limit collusion in resale, lead to earlier restructuring and higher output growth.

In the benchmark model, both the start of restructuring and the speed of transition are endogenous. But the outcome is not in doubt. Sooner or later, the economy is composed of efficient new private or restructured firms. Today, the notion that transition will indeed succeed seems plausible for most Central European countries. But, a few years into transition, when output was falling and un-employment rising, the outcome was more in doubt. The focus of much of the research was on potential derailments. Wouldn't the rise in unemployment lead to a fiscal crisis, or a political backlash? Might not state firms give up on restruc-turing and try again to extract subsidies, leading to the return of a soft budget constraint. Even today, these concerns are still relevant. Using potential derailments as a common theme, I look in Section 4.3 at various extensions of the benchmark model. I look in particular at the interactions between transition and fiscal policy.

4.1 A Benchmark Model

The model is a simplified version of Aghion and Blanchard [1994]. It has strong assumptions, in particular that the revenue product per worker is constant in both the state and private sectors. This makes it analytically tractable, indeed simple. Compared to a model which assumes more conventional and smoother technologies in both the state and private sectors, it leads however to results—such as two phases of transition, or discrete adjustments in response to changes in policy—that are idiosyncratic (in the sense that adjustment would be more gradual in a more conventional model). I shall point these out as I go along.[1]

4.1.1 The initial effects of reform

(1) The economy has two sectors, the state and the private sector. Pre-transition, there is no unemployment. State sector employment is large, private sector employment is small. Just after the start of reform—price liberalization, the elimination of subsidies to state firms—employment in state firms decreases, generating unemployment. The economy is as shown in Figure 4.1:

- Employment in the state sector is equal to N_s, with revenue product per worker equal to 1 (an innocuous normalization).
- Employment in the private sector is equal to N_p, with revenue product per worker equal to $(1 + \theta)$, with $\theta > 0$.
- The labour force is normalized to 1, so that unemployment, equivalently the unemployment rate, is given by $U = 1 - N_s - N_p$.

Let me make two remarks about these assumptions:

- In terms of the two-sector model presented in Chapter 2, I make in effect two specific assumptions: that technology is

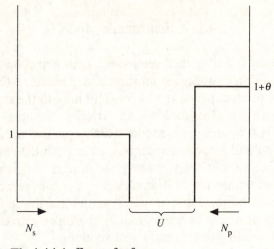

Fig. 4.1. The initial effects of reform

Leontief in labour and capital in both sectors; and that utility is linear in both goods. Together, these imply constant revenue products per worker in each sector, up to an amount determined by the capital stock in each sector. For unemployment to increase initially with the removal of subsidies, some capital must disappear/become obsolete in the state sector at the beginning of transition. Otherwise, there would be no unemployment under these assumptions after the removal of subsidies.

- The assumption of an instantaneous decrease in state sector employment is at clear variance with the facts. As we saw in Chapter 3, while subsidies were drastically decreased at the beginning of transition, firms were able to cushion this decrease through various means, from arrears to bank loans, leading to a more gradual decline in employment. I do not want to focus here on that aspect of transition. Ignoring it makes the model ill-suited to describe the early dynamics of transition; but the model is not misleading if the goal is to think about the medium term.

After this initial adjustment, the high revenue product per worker in the private sector leads to private employment creation, generating higher output, higher employment, and thus a flow out of unemployment. And, over time, state firms restructure, generating higher output as well as a flow of workers into unemployment. Let me look first at the determinants of private employment creation, then at the determinants of restructuring.

4.1.2 Private employment creation

The evolution of the new (as opposed to the privatized) private sector in Central Europe is one of the topics I did not look at in detail in Chapter 3. But the facts are reasonably clear. The private sector is growing. But it can only grow so fast: factors such as limited access to credit or lack of expertise are clearly constraining its growth.

(1) I formalize private employment creation as

$$H = a(1 + \theta - w), \tag{1.1}$$

where H is private employment creation (a flow), a is a parameter, $(1 + \theta)$ is the product per worker in the private sector, and w is the market wage. Thus, private employment creation depends on profit per worker, the difference between the average product of labour and the market wage. The higher the various constraints and adjustment costs facing the private sector, the lower is a.[2]

Equation (1.1) can be given two interpretations.

- The first is that it reflects costs of adjustment, from costs of installation of new capital, to constraints from limited expertise.[3]

  The assumption that technology is Leontief in capital and labour and the assumption that there are quadratic costs to investment would yield a forward-looking specification, with investment and employment creation depending on the present value of profits, rather than just current profit. We explored that specification in Aghion and Blanchard [1994]. I shall not do it here. On the balanced path below, profit is constant and this more general specification reduces to equation (1.1).

- The second is that it reflects financial constraints, such as, for example, the constraint that investment must be financed from retained earnings. A specification in which all cash flow was reinvested would lead, however, to a specification in terms of the rate of change—rather than the change—in private employment. This would capture the relevant notion that if the private sector is small to start with, it can only grow so fast. But it would complicate the analytics substantially, and thus I do not use a rate-of-change specification.[4]

(2) How is the market wage in turn determined? The general issue of market wage determination goes far beyond transition. Given my reading of labour market facts, my preference is for a theory of wage determination where the unemployed are worse off than the employed, and the wage depends on labour market conditions.

The simplest way of doing that is to assume that private firms set the wage in such a way that the value of being employed in the private sector exceeds the value of being unemployed by some amount c, which I take as exogenous here.[5] This assumption trivially implies that the unemployed are worse off than the employed. And it implies that the market wage depends on labour market conditions, even if the flow utility of being unemployed does not.

To see why, let V_p and V_u denote the values of being employed in the private sector and of being unemployed respectively. Characterizing the evolution of these values, together with the value of being employed in state firms, will prove essential in what follows, both here for wage determination, and below for restructuring decisions.[6] Assume that there is no turnover in either the private or the state sector; in that case, the flow out of unemployment is equal to hirings from the private sector, and the exit rate from unemployment is equal to (H/U).[7] The two values then satisfy the following 'arbitrage equations':

$$rV_u = b + (H/U)(V_p - V_u) + dV_u/dt, \qquad (1.2)$$

$$rV_p = w \qquad\qquad\qquad + dV_p/dt. \qquad (1.3)$$

When unemployed, a worker receives unemployment benefits b (I assume that the marginal utility of leisure is equal to 0), and has probability (H/U) of becoming employed and thus changing value from V_u to V_p. Thus, the flow value of being unemployed, rV_u, is equal to b plus $(H/U)(V_p - V_u)$, plus the expected change in the value of being unemployed. Similarly, when employed, a worker faces, by assumption, no risk of becoming unemployed again, and thus receives the market wage forever after. The flow value of being employed is equal to the wage plus the expected change in the value of being employed.[8]

The wage-setting condition is then the condition that firms set wages so that the value of being employed exceeds the value of being unemployed by an amount equal to c:

$$V_p = V_u + c. \qquad (1.4)$$

Taking the difference between equations (1.3) and (1.2), using equation (1.4), and noting that equation (1.4) also implies that $dV_p/dt = dV_u/dt$, gives the market wage

$$w = b + c(r + H/U). \qquad (1.5)$$

The market wage depends on unemployment benefits and labour market conditions. The correct indicator of labour market conditions is not the unemployment rate, but rather the exit rate out of unemployment (which, you will remember from Chapter 3, is extremely low in most Central European countries).

(3) Replacing the wage in equation (1.1) by its value from (1.5), and solving out gives both the market wage and private employment creation as a function of unemployment

$$w = \frac{ca}{(U+ca)}(1+\theta) + \frac{U}{(U+ca)}(b+cr) \qquad (1.6)$$

and

$$H = \frac{aU}{(U+ca)}(1+\theta-(b+cr)). \qquad (1.7)$$

Note that $(1 + \theta)$, the product per worker, is the highest wage a firm can pay and not make losses; $(b + cr)$ is the lowest wage the firm may want to pay, the wage corresponding to a labour market in which the exit rate from unemployment is 0. I shall assume that $(1 + \theta)$ exceeds $(b + cr)$: otherwise the private sector would never be viable. In that case, the wage is a decreasing function of the unemployment rate; and by implication, private employment creation is an increasing function of the unemployment rate.

This gives us the first half of the model: *Private employment creation depends on the profit rate. The profit rate depends in part on the wage. The wage is a decreasing function of un-employment. Thus, other things being equal, higher unemployment leads to higher private employment creation.*[9]

4.1.3 Restructuring of state firms

(1) In thinking about restructuring, I follow closely the discussion in Chapter 3. I assume that restructuring requires expertise and capital, and thus requires outside ownership. It is therefore associated with both technological and owner-ship/wage-setting changes.

The technological changes are as follows. Each state firm has a mass of workers equal to 1, each producing 1. Re-structuring leads to:

- an increase in the product per worker from 1 to $(1 + \theta)$ (It is unimportant that this be the same level as in the private sector; this just saves on notation, since I need to keep track only of 'the' private sector, new or privatized.);
- a decrease in the number of workers from 1 to $\lambda < 1$, so that

$(1 - \lambda)$ of the workers become unemployed. After restructuring, the firm thus produces $\lambda(1 + \theta)$ units of output. I shall assume that $\lambda(1 + \theta) \geq 1$, so that restructuring increases output while it decreases employment.

Again, these assumptions can be derived from an explicit treatment of technology. If technology is Leontief in capital and labour, and restructuring takes the form of labour-saving technological progress (for example, as discussed in Chapter 2, a reduction in labour due to the elimination of labour hoarding), then restructuring leads to the two effects above, with $\lambda(1 + \theta) = 1$.

The change in ownership implies a change in wage setting. The natural assumption here is that, after privatization, workers who are kept on receive the market wage, w, the same wage as in new private firms, so that the value of remaining employed in the restructured firm is equal to V_p. Those who are laid off are unemployed, with value V_u. I consider for the moment the case of pure outsider privatization, so that the workers do not receive shares in the new privatized firm.

(2) Restructuring is a decision taken by the workers in the firm. It takes place if workers expect to be at least as well off under restructuring as under the status quo.

More precisely, let V_s be the value of remaining employed in a non-restructured state firm. Recall that the revenue per worker in state firms absent restructuring is equal to 1. Thus, V_s satisfies the following arbitrage equation:

$$rV_s = 1 + \mathrm{d}V_s/\mathrm{d}t. \tag{1.8}$$

Then, given that restructuring leads to lay-offs of $(1 - \lambda)$ workers, and that the remaining λ workers are paid the market wage, workers will choose restructuring if and only if

$$V_s \leq \lambda V_p + (1 - \lambda)V_u. \tag{1.9}$$

Since V_s does not depend on the unemployment rate, and both V_p and V_u are decreasing in the unemployment rate, this implies that there is a critical unemployment rate, U^*, at which restructuring becomes attractive.[10]

This gives us the second half of the model: *Restructuring of state firms implies both an increase in output and an increase in unemployment. The decision to restructure depends, among other things, on the state of the labour market: the higher the unemployment rate, the less likely restructuring is to take place.*

4.1.4 The nature of transition

We can now put the two halves of the model together. I focus on the analytics in this subsection, on the economic interpretation and the implications in the next.

Given the interactions between private sector employment creation, restructuring, and unemployment, the transition path implied by this model has the following shape:

- If initial unemployment is below some critical value, U^*, then some restructuring takes place instantaneously until unemployment is equal to U^*. Transition then takes place at the constant unemployment rate U^*, with the flow of lay-offs from restructuring equal to the flow of hirings in the new private sector. In other words, the economy jumps to a balanced transition path, and stays there until the end of transition.
- If initial unemployment is above U^*—the case which I believe to be more relevant—then there is no restructuring until private employment creation has decreased unemployment down to U^*. At that point, the flow of restructuring starts, and the economy follows a balanced transition path, with unemployment remaining constant at U^* until the end of transition.

Let me characterize w^*, U^*, and s^*, the equilibrium wage, unemployment, and speed of restructuring along the balanced transition path.

Along the transition path associated with U^*, all variables which affect the values V_s, V_u, V_p are constant (only the composition of employment is changing), so that all three values are constant.[11]

From equation (1.8), the value of being employed in a state firm absent restructuring is given by

$$rV_s = 1. \tag{1.10}$$

From equations (1.2) and (1.3), and the condition that $V_p = V_u + c$, the values of being unemployed and of being employed in the private sector respectively are given by

$$rV_p = w,$$
$$rV_u = w - cr.$$

When the restructuring condition (1.9) holds as an equality, replacing the values by their expressions above gives

$$1 = \lambda w + (1 - \lambda)(w - cr). \tag{1.11}$$

If restructuring takes place, then with probability λ, workers receive the market wage; with probability $(1 - \lambda)$, they find themselves unemployed, and get the reservation wage, which is equal to the wage minus cr.

Solving for the market wage on the balanced path gives

$$w^* = 1 + (1 - \lambda)cr. \tag{1.12}$$

The market wage must be sufficiently attractive for workers in the state sector to be willing to restructure. In particular, given the risk that workers become unemployed, the market wage must exceed what workers currently receive in state firms.[12]

Recall that the market wage is a decreasing function of unemployment. Thus, equation (1.12) implicitly defines equilibrium unemployment. Unemployment must be such that, through its effect on the market wage and the reservation wage, workers in state firms are willing to take the risks associated with restructuring, so that equation (1.12) holds. Using equation (1.6), and solving out for equilibrium unemployment, gives[13]

$$U^* = ca\frac{(\theta - (1-\lambda)cr)}{(1-b-\lambda cr)}. \tag{1.13}$$

The equilibrium speed of restructuring, s^*, must be such that the flow into unemployment, which is equal to s^* times the proportion of workers laid off, $(1-\lambda)$, is equal to the flow out of unemployment, which is itself equal to private employment creation, H, when the wage is equal to w^*. Thus, s^* satisfies

$$s^*\lambda = a(\theta - (1-\lambda)cr). \tag{1.14}$$

Finally, note that, from equations (1.4) and (1.9), along the balanced path, all three values—the value of being employed in a state firm, V_s, the value of being employed in a private firm, V_p, and the value of being unemployed, V_u—are constant and equal to

$$\begin{aligned} V_p &= (1/r) + (1-\lambda)c, \\ V_s &= (1/r), \\ V_u &= (1/r) - \lambda c. \end{aligned} \tag{1.15}$$

Those employed in the private sector are best off, those unemployed are worst off. Those employed in state firms are in between. What changes along the balanced transition path are the proportions of workers in each category. The proportion of workers employed in private firms steadily increases, the proportion of workers in state firms steadily decreases, and the proportion of unemployed remains constant until the end of transition.

4.1.5 Implications

(1) This benchmark model gives a stark picture of transition: if the initial effects of reform lead to high unemployment, the economy goes through a first phase where no restructuring takes place. Depressed labour market conditions, and the risk of a long stay in unemployment and of a low market wage, lead workers in state firms to oppose restructuring.

During that period, the action only comes from private employment creation, which decreases unemployment over time.

As unemployment decreases, it eventually reaches the point where there is no longer opposition to restructuring in state firms. From then on, transition takes place both through private employment creation and restructuring of state firms. Output therefore increases faster than in the first phase, while unemployment now remains constant.

The two-phase nature of the solution is an artifact of the strong assumptions about technology and tastes (namely, Leontief technologies and linear utility). If we had assumed instead a distribution of initial average products across state firms, then there would be some restructuring from the start, and the rate of restructuring would be a smoother function of unemployment. But the basic message would remain: the higher initial unemployment, the less cumulative restructuring there would be at any point in time during the transition.

(2) The model points to the importance of two factors in shaping the dynamics of transition.

The first is the size of the initial shock, and the induced level of initial unemployment. The higher the initial rate of unemployment, the stronger and the longer-lasting the opposition to restructuring, and thus the slower the growth of output.

The second is the strength of private employment creation (which is captured by the value of the parameter a here). The stronger private employment creation, the shorter the initial phase of no restructuring. And the faster the speed of restructuring along the balanced transition path thereafter: from equation (1.14), note that every job created in the new private sector triggers restructuring of $(1/\lambda)$ jobs in state firms.

These two implications are, I believe, very relevant. Bulgaria provides a case in point. The initial shock led to a high rate of unemployment. This in turn has led to strong opposition to restructuring and outsider privatization, at both the firm and the national level. As a result of high unemployment and poor private sector growth, the pace of reform has slowed to a crawl.[14] Thus, one can expect a long period of high unemployment, and only limited restructuring and growth for some time to come.

4.2 Policies and Transition

I have built three explicit distortions into the model.[15] The first two would be present in any economy. The first is the presence of unemployment benefits. The second is the efficiency wage assumption, which implies that the wage is higher than unemployment benefits by an amount which depends on labour market conditions. The third is specific to transition; it is the assumption that workers have control rights but not property rights. This leads in turn to a distortion in the decision of whether to accept outsider privatization and restructuring.

Absent these distortions, the adjustment under the other assumptions I have made about technology would be as follows. The state sector would restructure at once, leading to a further increase in unemployment. The wage would be equal to 0 so long as there was unemployment (recall that I have assumed that the marginal utility of leisure is equal to 0). Private employment creation would then proceed at rate $H = a(1 + \theta)$ until unemployment had disappeared. There would, therefore, be strong distribution effects, with zero wages until the transition was completed.

By choosing the level of unemployment benefits and privatization rules, the government has a direct effect on two of the three distortions. And both the generosity of the safety net and the form of privatization have been the subject of intense political debate throughout the transition. In the rest of this section, I look at their effects in the benchmark model, and draw tentative policy implications.

4.2.1 Unemployment benefits

In many Central European countries, unemployment benefit rules were rather generous at the very beginning of transition. In all countries, the rules have now been considerably tightened, and are typically less generous than in Western European countries with similar unemployment rates.[16]

Obviously the main motivation for putting in place unemployment benefits is distributional, namely to make sure that those who become and remain unemployed through no fault of their own have enough to live on. It has been argued, however, that, in the context of transition, there may be an efficiency argument for unemployment benefits as well. If the risk of unemployment is what leads workers in state firms to oppose restructuring, then it would seem that higher unemployment benefits can decrease this opposition, and accelerate transition.[17] With this question in mind, let us look at the effects of unemployment benefits in the benchmark model.

(1) Look first at the effects of higher benefits on the balanced transition path. The level of benefits does not appear in equations (1.12) and (1.14); it follows that higher benefits have no effect on the market wage, w^*, and thus on the speed of restructuring, s^*. From equation (1.13), an increase in benefits leads to an increase in the unemployment rate, U^*. Furthermore, from equation (1.15), all three values—the values of being employed in either sector, or of being unemployed—are unaffected by unemployment benefits.

These results are basically Harris–Todaro results (Harris and Todaro 1970). More generous unemployment benefits indeed make it more attractive to restructure and take the risk of becoming unemployed. But they do not make it more attractive for the new private sector to hire. Thus, the outcome is an increase in unemployment until the exit rate from unemployment has fallen enough that the utility of being unemployed is the same as before. In other words, for those unemployed, higher utility from higher benefits is exactly offset by the decreased probability of getting a job.

(2) Turn now to the time it takes for the economy to reach the point where restructuring starts. Assume that initial unemployment is higher than U^*, so that there is no restructuring initially. There is only private employment creation, which decreases unemployment over time.

The higher value of U^* implies that it will take less of a decrease in unemployment from the initial level for restructuring to start. This is the sense in which higher benefits indeed have a positive effect on restructuring. If benefits are generous, restructuring will start when unemployment is still relatively high.

This, however, does not necessarily imply that restructuring will start earlier. This is because, before the economy reaches the balanced path, higher benefits lead to higher wages and thus to lower private employment creation; this follows from equation (1.7). Whether the effect of higher U^* or that of lower H dominates is ambiguous. If the effect of wages on private employment creation is small (maybe because other constraints, such as credit, play a dominant role), then higher unemployment benefits will indeed hasten restructuring. But if the wage effects on private sector growth are stronger, the effect may go the other way.

In terms of their effects on utility, unemployment benefits have a more conventional effect. Until the balanced path is reached, higher benefits lead to higher wages, and thus to higher values of being unemployed, or of being employed in the private sector.

The model therefore indicates that the case for increasing unemployment benefits on efficiency grounds is limited. It is non-existent once the economy is on the balanced transition path; it is ambiguous before the economy reaches the balanced path. This I believe to be a fairly robust result (which actually runs against my prior: I thought that the partial equilibrium argument would remain in general equilibrium and that one could make a stronger case for benefits as a way of accelerating restructuring).

And within the logic of the model, which only distinguishes between three states (employed in one or the other sector, or unemployed), the case for unemployment benefits on distributional grounds (between the employed and the unemployed) is also limited. They only improve the utility of the unemployed before the economy reaches the balanced transition path. On the balanced path, unemployment benefits have no effect on utility. Their beneficial effect is offset by the increase in equilibrium unemployment. This, however, I see more as a shortcoming of the model than a robust result. To the extent that labour market conditions differ very much across regions (as we saw in Chapter 3), the high-unemployment regions are likely to be in the first phase of transition for a long time. And to the extent that the unemployed differ in their exit rates, then unemployment benefits will help those with the lowest exit rates, thus those who are likely to need it the most.[18]

4.2.2 Privatization rules

In the benchmark model, I assumed pure outsider privatization: workers received no shares in the restructured/ privatized firm. But, as we saw in Chapter 3, whether and how much of a stake workers should have in privatized firms has been one of the main debates of the transition.

The debate has fiscal, distributional, and efficiency dimensions. More generous terms given to insiders decrease potential revenues from privatization (although these have turned out to be small in any case). They obviously favour insiders in state firms over the rest of the population, and to the extent that state firms differ in value, favour insiders differentially. They affect the incentives of workers and managers to support or fight restructuring. I shall limit myself to this third dimension, and look at the effects of rules which give more generous terms to insiders on the

speed of restructuring and the evolution of output in our
model. In doing so, I shall build on the partial equilibrium
analysis of Chapter 3.

Assume that workers are given a proportion α of shares in
the firm. Pure outsider privatization, the case we considered
in the benchmark model, corresponds to $\alpha = 0$. Pure insider
privatization corresponds to $\alpha = 1$. The question I now take
up is: How will the value of α affect the path of transition?

Start with the restructuring decision. For notational
convenience, assume the market wage to be constant over
time (the arguments extend straightforwardly to the case
where the market wage varies over time; the only cost is
added notation, coming from the use of present values of
flows, rather than the flows themselves.) Extending the argument underlying equation (1.11) earlier, restructuring will
take place if and only if

$$1 \leq \lambda w + (1 - \lambda)(w - cr) + \alpha\lambda(1 + \theta - w). \qquad (2.1)$$

The new term (compared to equation (1.11)) is the third one
on the right, which captures the profits going to each initial
worker under restructuring: $(1 + \theta - w)$ is the profit per
worker in the restructured firm; there are λ workers in the
restructured firm; the initial workers receive a share α of
total profits. Since this last term is positive, the inequality is
more likely to hold. Thus, and rather obviously, the more
they benefit from restructuring, the more willing workers
will be to restructure.[19]

Turn now to the general equilibrium implications. Given
equation (2.1), the values of the wage, speed of transition,
and the unemployment rate along the balanced transition
path are given by

$$w^* = 1 + (1 - \lambda)cr + \alpha\lambda(1 + \theta - w^*),$$
$$s^*\lambda = a(1 + \theta - w^*),$$
$$U^* = ca(1 + \theta - w^*)/(w^* - b - cr).$$

Thus, on the balanced path, an increase in α decreases the market wage, increases the speed of transition, and increases unemployment.

Suppose that the economy starts with initial unemployment above U^*. Before the economy reaches the balanced path, no restructuring takes place, and thus privatization rules have no impact on private employment creation. The fact that U^* is higher implies, however, that it takes less time for unemployment to reach U^*, and for restructuring to start.

Thus, from an efficiency point of view, privatization rules which are more generous to insiders are highly desirable. They lead restructuring to start earlier, and lead to both higher private employment creation and a higher speed of restructuring thereafter. The difference with unemployment benefits is striking. For given labour market conditions, both policies make it more appealing to restructure. But, along the balanced transition path, unemployment benefits do not affect the market wage and thus do not affect private employment creation and the speed of restructuring. More generous privatization rules on the other hand lead to a lower market wage, and thus to both higher private employment creation and higher speed of restructuring: for workers in state firms, lower market wages are offset by a higher stake in restructured firms.

The efficiency gain comes at a distributional cost. The values of being employed in a state firm, or of becoming employed in a private firm, or of becoming unemployed, taking into account the fact that those who change status as a result of restructuring receive a share of profits, are all independent of α. But, those who are unemployed or employed in the private sector and were not working in state firms earlier—and therefore are not receiving a share of the profits—are now worse off. General equilibrium effects are quite different from partial equilibrium effects; but they also imply that those not working in state firms lose from more generous privatization rules.

4.3 Derailments, and Other Extensions

In the benchmark model, transition may take more or less time, come with more or less unemployment. But it eventually succeeds: state firms are restructured, and the economy ends up in private efficient hands. Such a rosy scenario looks more plausible today than it did a few years into transition, when output was still declining and unemployment rapidly increasing. But it may still be too optimistic a view of transition. There were indeed risks of derailment, and not all have disappeared. They can be roughly put into three categories.

In the benchmark model, absent restructuring, state firms can survive indefinitely. This is surely too optimistic. Absent restructuring, state firms are more likely to die slowly, losing markets, losing crucial workers, even losing opportunities for restructuring. This raises the possibility that high unemployment prevents restructuring, leading to more unemployment.

In the benchmark model, the average product of labour in the private sector is unaffected by developments in the state sector. This assumption is crude. Private firms may learn and grow by acting as suppliers to state firms; if state firms do poorly, such opportunities may be lost. The profit of private firms is likely to depend on the size of the market: the scope for retail trade is definitely more limited in a town where the state firm has just closed. Thus, lack of restructuring in state firms may well make it harder for the private sector to grow. High unemployment may not only prevent restructuring, but also slow down private employment creation.

Finally, the benchmark model ignores fiscal interactions. I have assumed implicitly that unemployment benefits were financed by lump-sum taxation. Governments in transition —or elsewhere—do not have access to lump-sum taxation. Higher spending must lead to higher taxes, or to cuts in spending elsewhere, or to higher debt or money creation.

Higher taxes, or lower spending on infrastructure investment, may hinder private employment creation. Higher
money creation and inflation can have equally adverse
effects.

The issues go beyond just the budget constraint of the
government, and take us into the realm of political economy.
If, for example, firms face the choice of restructuring or
lobbying for subsidies, higher unemployment and thus a
higher private cost of restructuring may lead them to spend
more of their time lobbying and possibly obtaining subsidies. Through these narrow and political-economic fiscal
feedbacks, unemployment may derail the transition.

In the rest of this section, I examine two of these
possibilities. I examine first the implications of the slow
death of state firms absent restructuring, and look, in that
context, at the evolution of the support for reform along the
transition path. I then examine the implications of financing
unemployment benefits through taxes on employment. I
then compare the implications of the model to the evolution
of fiscal policy in Bulgaria and the Czech Republic.

4.3.1 Slow death of state firms

Assume that, absent restructuring, state firms die with
instantaneous probability π. Then, absent restructuring, the
evolution of employment in state firms follows

$$\mathrm{d}N_s/\mathrm{d}t = -\pi N_s.$$

And V_s, the value of remaining in a non-restructured state
firm now satisfies

$$rV_s = x + \pi(V_u - V_s) + \mathrm{d}V_s/\mathrm{d}t.$$

The new term, $\pi(V_u - V_s)$, is equal to the probability that the
firm dies times the change in value from becoming unemployed.

If π is small, and if the labour market is sufficiently depressed, workers may still prefer not to restructure. A small

probability of death may well dominate the immediacy of the risks associated with restructuring. The transition will then look as follows.

Suppose that the economy starts with high initial unemployment, so that workers do not want to restructure. As state firms slowly die, the flow into unemployment is equal to πN_s. If this flow initially exceeds private employment creation, unemployment will keep increasing, reinforcing the opposition to restructuring.

Can unemployment increase forever, and transition derail? Not under these assumptions. Unemployment may increase for some time, but eventually things will turn around. As the size of the state sector declines, so does the flow into unemployment. At some point, this flow becomes smaller than private sector employment creation, and unemployment starts decreasing. Eventually unemployment becomes low enough that restructuring becomes attractive. From then on, the economy continues on the same balanced path as in the benchmark model, with both private employment creation and restructuring.

In short, if state firms that do not restructure die slowly, transition may lead to a long period of high unemployment, during which there is no restructuring. While private employment creation implies that unemployment eventually comes down, and restructuring eventually starts, this may come very late. By then, most state firms may have died.

It is interesting to trace what happens to the welfare of the various groups along the transition path, as measured by the various present values of utility (the V's) in the model.

- As unemployment increases initially, welfare may well go down for all groups, especially for those who are either unemployed or employed in the private sector.[20] The unemployed and those in the private sector suffer directly from depressed labour market conditions. Those employed in the state sector suffer only because of the risk that the firm dies and that they find themselves unemployed.

- And, as unemployment increases and the private sector expands, the proportion of workers either unemployed or employed in the private sector also increases. Thus, on both counts, the support for reform may go down for some time, before eventually recovering as unemployment decreases and welfare increases again for all groups.[21]

This variation on the benchmark model can thus explain the broadly U-shaped evolution of Polish public opinion we saw in Figure 1.11 in Chapter 1. I suspect, however, that more has been at work. It is hard not to interpret the initial optimism about the future in Figure 1.11 (and its rapid decline thereafter) as reflecting incorrect expectations, or at least a very optimistic prior about the effects of reform.

4.3.2 The government budget constraint

To show the potential effects of fiscal feedbacks, this second extension adds a crude government budget constraint and distortionary taxation to the benchmark model.[22]

(1) Suppose that the only form of government spending is unemployment benefits, that the government runs a balanced budget, and that benefits are financed through an employment tax levied on both state and private firms. Let the tax per worker be equal to z. The government budget constraint is thus given by

$$(1 - U)z = Ub. \qquad (3.1)$$

$(1 - U)$ is total employment in state and private firms. The tax per worker, z, must be such that tax revenues, $(1 - U)z$, cover total unemployment benefits, Ub. This equation has a straightforward implication: higher unemployment requires a higher tax rate. The effect is non-linear. As unemployment increases, the amount to be financed increases, and the tax base (employment) decreases; as unemployment tends towards 1, the tax rate tends towards infinity.

Modifications to the rest of the model are straight-forward. Profit per worker in the private sector is equal to $(1 + \theta - w - z)$, so that a higher tax rate leads to lower profit, and thus lower private sector employment creation. Using equation (3.1) to eliminate z, equation (1.7) becomes

$$H = \frac{aU}{(U+ca)}(1+\theta - (b\frac{1}{1-U} + cr)). \qquad (3.2)$$

Unemployment now has two effects on H. First, and as before, higher unemployment leads to lower wages and faster employment creation; this effect is captured by the first fraction in equation (3.2). Second, higher unemployment leads to higher taxes, and thus lower employment creation; this effect is captured in the second fraction. It is easy to check that the first effect dominates at low unemployment, and the second dominates at high unemployment. Let me denote the relation between hirings and unemployment by $H(U)$ in what follows; $H'(U)$ is positive for low unemployment, negative for high unemployment.

As in the first extension, I assume that, absent restructuring, state firms die at rate π, so that, absent restructuring, the dynamics of state sector employment and of unemployment are given by:

$$dN_s/dt = -\pi N_s,$$
$$dU/dt = \pi N_s - H(U).$$

State employment decreases over time at rate π. And the change in unemployment is equal to the flow from state employment due to the death of state firms minus the flow of hirings by the private sector.

Finally, the presence of taxes also slightly modifies the restructuring decision: the wage absent restructuring is now equal to $(1 - z)$, rather than 1 as before. Given the average product of labour, higher unemployment implies a higher tax and thus a lower after-tax wage absent restructuring. This makes it less attractive not to restructure.

The basic implications of this extended model are easy to

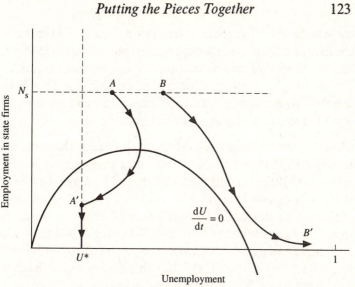

Fig. 4.2. Dynamics under fiscal feedbacks: how transition can fail

characterize. There is again an unemployment rate, U^*, such that, if unemployment is equal to U^*, workers in state firms are willing to restructure, and the economy proceeds on a balanced transition path. But, now, we cannot be sure that unemployment will ever decrease to U^*.

To see why, consider the phase diagram in Figure 4.2. The shape of the locus $(dU/dt = 0)$, or equivalently $N_s = H(U)/\pi$, derives from the shape of the function $H(U)$: at low unemployment, increases in unemployment increase private employment creation. At high unemployment, they decrease it, and eventually make it negative. Above the locus $(dU/dt = 0)$, unemployment increases. Below it, it decreases.

Given initial state employment N_s, Figure 4.2 shows two potential paths of transition. In the first, denoted AA', unemployment increases for a while. But it then starts decreasing, until it gets to point A', where restructuring starts and transition continues on the balanced transition path. In the second, denoted BB', unemployment keeps increasing until it reaches 1: transition derails. The cause is the fiscal feedback. As unemployment increases, so do taxes, leading to weaker and weaker private employment creation. Private employment creation never exceeds the flow into unemployment from the death of state firms, and unemployment keeps increasing until it reaches 1.[23]

(2) How have countries actually handled these fiscal feedbacks? How much of a role have they played in the transition? Bulgaria and the Czech Republic make for a nice study in contrasts here.

Start with Bulgaria. The evolution of its fiscal position since 1989 is summarized in Table 4.1. From 1989 to 1992, explicit subsidies to state firms were slashed from 15.5 per cent to 1.8 per cent of GDP. But this decrease in subsidies was much more than offset by a drop in revenues from 59.8 per cent to 38.3 per cent of GDP. Most of this drop was due in turn to the factors we discussed in Chapter 3, the drop in

Table 4.1. Bulgaria: revenues and expenditures (percentage of GDP)

	1989	1990	1991	1992	1993	1994
Total revenue	59.8	51.6	40.4	38.3	35.2	38.0
Profit tax	23.2	17.9	16.5	8.4	5.4	7.2
Turnover/excise taxes	12.0	10.0	8.2	8.3	10.3	13.1
Total expenditures	61.5	60.4	55.0	53.4	50.9	45.0
Goods and services	24.1	22.5	17.6	18.7	17.5	15.2
Interest payments	3.1	5.6	17.9	15.9	14.2	14.1
Social security benefits	10.4	12.0	13.7	14.3	15.2	12.9
Subsidies	15.5	14.9	4.2	1.8	2.2	1.3
Capital expenditures	5.5	3.1	2.0	2.8	1.9	1.5
Deficit	1.7	8.8	14.6	15.1	15.7	7.0

Source: IMF [1996].

output, and the appropriation of profits by workers in state firms, leading to the disappearance of accounting profits and of profit taxes. From 1989 to 1992, profit taxes declined by 14.8 per cent of GDP.

This drop in revenues was further compounded by the effects of increasing unemployment. In Bulgaria as elsewhere in Central Europe, unemployment benefits were substantially tightened as unemployment increased. Thus, the direct effect of the increase in unemployment on unemployment benefits was more limited than in the model I sketched above. But, thanks to generous retirement rules, one of the ways employment was reduced was through a sharp increase in early retirements. The ratio of pensioners to employed workers, which had stood at 58 per cent in 1990, increased to 86 per cent in 1993! This was reflected in an increase in social security benefits, from 10.4 per cent in 1989 to 15.2 per cent of GDP in 1993 (as Table 4.1 shows). Only since 1994 have these benefits been reduced as well.

How did the government adjust to these two adverse fiscal shocks? First, by allowing for a large budget deficit (although the inflation-adjusted deficit has been much smaller than the numbers reported in Table 4.1: Budina and van Wijnbergen [1995] estimate that the 1993 adjusted deficit was 2.9 per cent, and that Bulgaria actually ran an adjusted surplus of 5 per cent in 1994). Second, by cutting capital expenditures. Capital expenditures decreased from 5.5 per cent of GDP in 1989 to 1.5 per cent of GDP in 1994. In view of the dilapidated state of infrastructure, and the importance of infrastructure for attracting foreign investment, this is surely one of the factors which explains the very low level of FDI in Bulgaria (a cumulative 2 per cent of 1994 GDP) since the start of transition.

Contrast the experience of Bulgaria with that of the Czech Republic, shown in Table 4.2. In the Czech Republic, transition was also associated with a dramatic decrease in subsidies, from 25 per cent of GDP in 1989 to less than 3.4

Table 4.2. Czech Republic: revenues and expenditures (percentage of GDP)

	1989	1990	1991	1992	1993	1994
Total revenue	69.5	61.1	55.0	48.3	50.4	51.2
Profit tax	11.0	12.2	13.7	10.6	7.7	6.2
Turnover/VAT	19.5	21.2	13.8	12.5	13.3	14.4
Total expenditures	72.3	61.5	57.1	47.5	49.4	50.7
Goods and services	25.2	24.6	24.4	20.2	23.2	25.1
Interest payments	0.0	0.2	0.5	1.0	1.6	1.4
Social security benefits	13.6	13.6	16.1	14.0	13.8	13.7
Subsidies	25.0	16.2	7.7	5.0	3.9	3.4
Capital expenditures	8.5	6.9	8.4	7.3	6.7	7.1
Deficit	2.8	0.4	2.1	–0.8	–1.0	–0.5

Note: Until 1991, the numbers are for Czechoslovakia.

Source: IMF [1996].

per cent of GDP in 1994. But, in contrast to Bulgaria, this decrease in expenditures was not offset by the decrease in revenues. As we saw in Chapter 3, profits did not collapse in state firms in the Czech Republic, and thus profit taxes in particular remained high. Only since 1993 have they started declining. These developments have allowed the Czech Republic to maintain a small budget surplus and a high level of capital expenditures.

Can the differences in fiscal policy between Bulgaria and the Czech Republic be explained fully through the response to different economic situations? Surely not. But economic conditions have played an important role. There is no question for example that the economic situation forced the Bulgarian government to limit the deficit by cutting, among other things, public investment. And there is also no question that low public investment is hindering foreign direct investment and private employment creation.

4.4 Conclusions

(1) I have developed in this book a way of thinking about transition. I have argued that the two central mechanisms shaping transition have been reallocation (from old to new activities, from existing to new firms) and restructuring (of existing state firms). I have shown how the interactions between private employment creation, restructuring of state firms, and unemployment can explain the U-shaped response of output, the large increase in unemployment, and the low levels of investment which have characterized transition in Central Europe.

(2) I have tried all along to explain differences between the transition paths of Central European countries, and more casually, between Central Europe and countries to the East, from Russia to China. I feel I have made some progress. For example, how worse initial conditions have slowed down transition in Bulgaria is fairly clear. So is the role of differences in safety nets in explaining the different employment experiences of Central Europe and Russia. Some puzzles remain. I do not have a good explanation, for example, for why the same decline in output has led to less employment decline in the Czech Republic than in other Central European countries, despite an apparently larger role of managers and more progress on privatization.

(3) I have looked at the role of policies in transition. Some policies are clearly better than others. For example, the analysis strongly suggests that carefully designed insider privatization is the best way to achieve restructuring of state firms in the long run. I have not come up, however, with a simple list of good or bad policies, or a simple judgement as to whether big-bang policies are better than gradualism. Those in positions of power must construct simple messages and ignore ambiguities. Our models rarely generate such

simple messages. The analysis of transition is very much an analysis of the second-best, and comes with the typical attendant ambiguities.

Take the case for or against subsidies to state firms. Surely one of the most widely agreed-upon recommendations to governments in transition economies has been to harden the budget constraint of state firms. But this book has presented a number of intellectually respectable arguments for maintaining at least some subsidies for some time. A commitment to maintaining state firms for some time may avoid some of the disorganization effects we saw in Chapter 2. If high unemployment hinders rather than helps private employment creation, subsidies may limit the rise of unemployment and thus help private sector employment creation.[24] Or take the case for balancing the budget. If the private sector is credit constrained, it may actually be optimal to avoid taxing it until it has grown, and, if necessary, accumulate debt along the way.

In the end, political-economic considerations may well imply that the only credible level of subsidies is 0, and that the only credible fiscal policy is one which balances the budget. It may well be that, if transition comes with an early window of 'extraordinary politics', that window should be used to pass reforms which are stronger than is optimal in our models. But we should still be aware of the complexities of the arguments, and this is what models are for.

(4) I have stayed away from forecasts and growth predictions. Comparisons with fast-growing Asian countries are useful here but can only go so far.[25] One can, however, identify the problems that Central European countries will have to solve in order to continue growing at the current high rates.

In many countries, privatization is far from achieved. Privatization rules have to be designed so that they actually lead to privatization and restructuring. As restructuring takes place, governments have to brace themselves for closures of large firms and large plants, an end-game which has proven difficult to play even in Western economies. If they are to keep growing, medium-sized private firms must have easier access to outside finance than they have had so far. The housing market must improve so as to allow for higher labour mobility and the reduction of regional unemployment differences through migration. And countries must avoid the risk that high long-term unemployment leads to the emergence of a culture of unemployment. I hope that the framework I have developed in this book can contribute to a better discussion of all of these issues.

NOTES

1. Among models that formalize transition as a joint process of adjustment of state firms and growth of a new private sector, the two closest are those developed by Chadha *et al.* [1993]—which differs mainly from this one in having smoother technologies, but a more primitive determination of wages—and, more recently, Commander and Tolstopiatenko [1996]. Brixova and Kiyotaki [1996] have a more explicit treatment of the expertise and credit constraints on private sector growth than here. Boeri [1996] focuses on the role of job-to-job flows, which are absent from this model, but, as we saw in Chapter 3, are very relevant in reality. Rodrik [1994] represents an interesting attempt at integrating such dynamic models and the political-economic models of reform. Other dynamic two-sector models of transition include Alexeev and Kaganovich [1995]; Katz and Owen [1993]. My own attempt at building a simulation model, with two sectors, with capital and labour, explicit wage setting in each sector, and restructuring decisions, is presented in Blanchard and Keeling [1996].

2. It will be clear below that the parameter *a* plays an important role in determining the path of transition: a higher value of *a* leads not only to faster private employment growth, but also to faster state firm restructuring, and thus to faster transition on two fronts. I take *a* as given here, but discussions with Andrei Shleifer have convinced me that looking at the determinants of

a might help explain some of the differences in the evolutions of output across countries. For example, corruption and the degree of competition for rents by government officials determine how much of the profits entrepreneurs get to keep, and thus how fast the private sector will grow (see Shleifer and Vishny 1993 for further discussion). Evidence from surveys of private entrepreneurs shows that corruption and rent extraction have played a much smaller role in Poland than in Russia (see Shleifer 1997). This begs in turn the question of where this difference may come from. This issue is also discussed in Shleifer [1997], but without full resolution.

3. Chadha *et al.* [1993] formalize the evolution of expertise over time as coming from learning by doing.

4. The technical complication is that employment in the private sector would become a state variable, increasing the dimension of the dynamic system by 1 and eliminating the constant unemployment, balanced transition path derived below. Chadha *et al.* [1993] and Blanchard and Keeling [1996] show the implications of the rate of change formalization.

5. The fact that the wage exceeds the reservation wage comes out, for example, from models where firms use the wage to deter shirking, such as Shapiro and Stiglitz [1984]. In that model, *c* depends in turn on the cost of effort by workers, and the probability of being caught if shirking. But I do not want to be wedded to a particular interpretation here.

6. Note that what I called the reservation wage and denoted v in Chapter 3 is formally given by rV_u, the flow value of being unemployed.

7. Allowing for a richer description of flows, in particular for the fact that there is turnover in the private sector, and that flows into employment are coming both from unemployment and employment, would be worth exploring (see Boeri 1996 for a start.) The technical issue is again an increase in the dimension of the implied dynamic system. For example, if turnover is larger in the private sector, how much total turnover there is in the economy will depend on the size of the private sector, and thus increase over time.

8. These two equations are just a convenient way of stating that V_u and V_p are the expected present values of current and future earnings, conditional on being either currently unemployed

(V_u), or currently employed (V_p). For those unfamiliar with such 'arbitrage' equations, an alternative way of thinking about and deriving them is to think of arbitrage (thus the name) between three assets, a riskless asset paying r, an asset paying an expected flow of payments in the future, conditional on being unemployed today, and an asset paying an expected flow of payments in the future, conditional on being employed today. Let V_u and V_p be the prices of the last two assets. The expected flow return from 'holding' V_u is equal to unemployment benefits, b, plus the probability of changing status times the difference between the value of being employed and the value of being unemployed, $(H/U)(V_p - V_u)$, plus the expected capital gain, (dV_u/dt). The expected rate of return from holding the asset is thus equal to $(b + (H/U) (V_p - V_u) + dV_u/dt)/V_u$. Arbitrage implies that this expected rate of return must be equal to the rate of return on the riskless asset, r. This equality yields equation (1.2). Similarly, 'holding' the third asset gives a flow return of $w + dV_p/dt$, and thus a rate of return of $(w + dV_p/dt)/V_p$. Equality between this rate of return and the riskless rate yields equation (1.3).

9. One can think of a number of reasons why high unemployment may not be conducive to private employment creation. I leave them aside for the moment, but I shall return to them in Section 4.3.

10. Note that equation (1.9) implicitly assumes that workers take decisions behind a veil of ignorance, so that they are identical ex ante, and compare expected utility under both alternatives. As we discussed in Chapter 3, the veil-of-ignorance assumption may be a poor description of reality. If for example, workers know whether they will or will not be laid off, and each voter has veto power, then restructuring will take place only if those who are sure to become unemployed are at least indifferent, thus if $V_s \le V_u$. In that case, the formal analysis below goes through with minor modifications. But, not surprisingly, it takes longer for restructuring to start, and unemployment is lower along the balanced path.

11. I cheat here by using in effect a turnpike approximation. Variables such as H and w are constant until restructuring comes to an end; when restructuring comes to an end however, the flow into unemployment stops, and unemployment

decreases asymptotically to 0 as a result of private job creation, affecting both H and w. This implies that the V's, which are forward-looking, change before the end of restructuring. Far away enough from the end, however, these anticipation effects are small. Thus, I ignore them in order to focus on a constant value of U^*.

12. Recall that, for the moment, I am assuming full outsider privatization, so that workers do not get shares from privatization.

13. I shall assume that $\theta \geq (1 - \lambda)cr$, so that U^* is positive. The interpretation of this condition is as follows. The highest wage that private firms can pay is $(1 + \theta)$. The lowest private wage such that workers in state firms are willing to restructure is $(1 + (1 - \lambda)cr)$. Thus the condition says that there is a private wage at which workers in state firms will be willing to restructure.

14. For example, the index of liberalization constructed by De Melo *et al.* [1995] shows the same large increase in Bulgaria in 1991 as in Poland in 1990. But since then, the index has barely increased.

15. The model is sufficiently agnostic about the origin of adjustment costs in the private sector that there may well be distortions hidden there as well, such as financial constraints. I shall ignore those here. They are made explicit in Brixova and Kiyotaki [1996].

16. See Chapter 3, and references therein.

17. The argument has been made in particular in the case of Russia, which has had an extremely limited safety net.

18. What matters here is how the exit rate of an individual changes with the aggregate exit rate. Take an unemployed worker who has no chance of finding a job, so that his exit rate is equal to 0. As we saw in the text, an increase in b will decrease the average exit rate, but will clearly leave his exit rate unaffected (still equal to 0). He will clearly be better off as a result of higher unemployment benefits.

19. As we saw in Chapter 3, even full insider privatization ($\alpha = 1$) may not however remove all distortions in the resale/restructuring decision. If the decision to sell the firm to outsiders is taken collectively, the wedge between the wage and the reservation wage may still prevent efficient restructuring. The

government can design insider privatization so as to avoid such collusion; if it does so, it will remove the wedge in the restructuring decision. I shall not repeat this discussion here.

20. The qualifier 'may' comes from the fact that, as workers look forward, expectations of better things to come may lead to an increase in the present value of utility flows even if unemployment is still increasing. With a sufficiently high discount rate, all three values will decline for some time.

21. Decreased support for reform may not mean the end of transition but may simply lead to grumbling or unhappiness. What happens will depend on the policy alternatives available to people, something that I have not specified in this model. The role of these alternatives, and the fact that the government can design policy so as to determine what these alternatives may be, and in so doing maintain support for reform, have been discussed in particular by Dewatripont and Roland [1992], or Roland [1996]. For some empirical evidence on the relation between unemployment and support for pro- and anti-reform parties during transition in Central Europe, see Fidrmuc [1996].

22. This extension is a modified version of Aghion and Blanchard [1994]. Other models which focus on fiscal feedbacks include Coricelli [1995], which focuses on the effects of alternative forms of taxation, and Ruggerone [1996], which focuses on the interaction between transition and inflation, through money finance of the deficit. In an interesting description of transition in China, Brandt and Zhu [1995] construct a model which focuses on the relation between credit to state firms, money finance, and inflation, and provides a tentative explanation for the cycles of growth and inflation which have characterized Chinese transition. Keeling [1996] shows that, if private firms are credit constrained, it may be optimal for the government to run a budget deficit for some time and stabilize the debt through higher taxes later, when the private sector has grown.

23. For a more detailed treatment, and a discussion of what happens when private firms are forward-looking, see Aghion and Blanchard [1994]. The earlier model differs, however, from this one in two ways. The first is that I take the rate of change rather than the change of state employment to be

constant here. The second is a difference of interpretation. In this model, the flow into unemployment comes from the lack of restructuring. In the earlier model, the flow represented the flow of lay-offs from restructuring, where the speed of restructuring was taken to be exogenous.

24. For a parallel discussion of the case for some protection early in transition, see Flemming [1993].
25. See Sachs and Warner [1996].

References

Aghion, P., and Blanchard, O., 1994, On the speed of transition in Central Europe, *NBER Macroeconomics Annual*, pp. 283–320.

—— 1996, On privatization methods in Eastern Europe and their implications, mimeo, MIT and EBRD.

Aghion, P., Blanchard, O., and Burgess, R., 1994, The behavior of state firms in Eastern Europe pre-privatization, *European Economic Review* 38(6): 132–49.

Alexeev, M., and Kaganovich, M., 1995, Dynamics of privatization under a subsistence constraint, mimeo, Indiana University.

Alfandari, G., and Schaffer, M., 1996, 'Arrears' in the Russian enterprise sector, pp. 87–139 in Simon Commander, Qimiao Fan, and Mark Schaffer (eds.), *Enterprise Restructuring and Economic Policy in Russia* (Washington, DC: EDI, World Bank).

Åslund, A., Boone, P., and Johnson, S., 1996, How to stabilize: lessons from post-communist countries, *Brookings Papers on Economic Activity* 1: 217–313.

Atkeson, A., and Kehoe, P., 1995, Industry evolution and transition: measuring investment in organization capital, mimeo, University of Pennsylvania.

Balcerowitz, L., 1994, Understanding postcommunist transition, *Journal of Democracy* 5(4): 75–89.

Balcerowitz, L., and Gelb, A., 1994, Macropolicies in transition to a market economy: a three-year perspective, *Annual Bank Conference on Development Economics* (Washington, DC: World Bank).

Baumol, W., 1967, Macroeconomics of unbalanced growth: the anatomy of urban crisis, *American Economic Review* 57: 415–26.

Belka, M., Estrin, S., Schaffer, M., and Singh, I., 1995, Enterprise adjustment in Poland: evidence from a survey of 200 private, privatized, and state-owned firms, CEP Discussion Paper 233 (London: LSE).

Bentolila, S., 1997, The labor market in Poland, mimeo, CEMFI, Madrid.

Berg, A., 1993, Measurement and mismeasurement of economic

activity during transition to a market, pp. 39–63 in *Eastern Europe in Transition: From Recession to Growth?* World Bank Discussion Papers 196 (Washington, DC: World Bank).

Berg, A., and Blanchard, O., 1994, Stabilization and transition in Poland: 1990–1991, pp. 51–92 in O. Blanchard, K. Froot, and J. Sachs (eds.), *The Transition in Eastern Europe*, vol. 1 (Chicago, IL: NBER and University of Chicago Press).

Blanchard, O., and Diamond, P., 1990, The cyclical behavior of the gross flows of US workers, *Brookings Papers on Economic Activity* 2: 85–155.

Blanchard, O., and Keeling, J., 1996, A numerical model of transition, mimeo, MIT.

Blanchard, O., and Kremer, M., 1997, Disorganization, *Quarterly Journal of Economics*, forthcoming.

Blanchard, O., Commander, S., and Coricelli F., 1995, *Unemployment and Restructuring in Eastern Europe*, pp. 289–330 in S. Commander and F. Coricelli (eds.), *Unemployment, Restructuring, and the Labor Market in Eastern Europe and Russia* (Washington, DC: World Bank).

Blanchard, O., Boycko, M., Dabrowski, M., Dornbusch, R., Layard, R., and Shleifer, A., 1993, *Post-Communist Reform: Pain and Progress* (Cambridge, MA: MIT Press).

Blanchflower, D., and Oswald, A., 1994, *The Wage Curve* (Cambridge, MA: MIT Press).

Boeri, T., 1995, Labour market flows and the scope of labour market policies in Central and Eastern Europe, mimeo, OECD.

—— 1996, Labor market flows in the midst of structural change, mimeo, OECD.

Boeri, T., and Scarpetta, S., 1994, Convergence and divergence of regional labour market dynamics in Central and Eastern Europe, mimeo, Vienna Institute for Advanced Studies.

Bonin, J., and Schaffer, M., 1995, Banks, firms, bad debts and bankruptcy in Hungary 1991–1994, CEP Discussion Paper 234 (London: LSE).

Borensztein, E., Demekas, D., and Ostry, J., 1993, An empirical analysis of the output decline in three Eastern European countries, *IMF Staff Papers* 40(1): 1–31.

Boycko, M., Shleifer, A., and Vishny, R., 1995, *Privatizing Russia* (Cambridge, MA: MIT Press).

Brandt, L., and Zhu, X., 1995, Soft budget constraints and

inflation cycles: a positive model of the post-reform Chinese economy, mimeo, Toronto.

Brixova, Z., and Kiyotaki, N., 1996, Private sector development in transition economies, mimeo, Minnesota and LSE.

Bruno, M., 1994, Stabilization and reform in Eastern Europe: a preliminary evaluation, pp. 19–51 in O. Blanchard, K. Froot, and J. Sachs (eds.), *The Transition in Eastern Europe* (Chicago, IL: NBER and University of Chicago Press).

Bruno, M., and Easterly, W., 1995, Could inflation stabilization be expansionary?, *Transition* 6 (July–August): 1–3 (Washington, DC: World Bank).

Bruno, M., and Sachs, J., 1985, *The Economics of Worldwide Stagflation* (Oxford: Basil Blackwell).

Budina, N., and van Wijnbergen, S., 1995, Fiscal deficits, monetary reform and inflation in transition economies: the case of Bulgaria, mimeo, University of Amsterdam.

Carlin, W., Van Reenan, J., and Wolfe, T., 1994, Enterprise restructuring in the transition: an analytical survey of the case study evidence from Central and Eastern Europe, EBRD Working Paper 14.

Centrum Badania Opinii Spolecznej, 1993, *Oczekiwania zwiazane z przeksztalceniami wlasnosciowymi i ich konfrontacja z rzeczywistoscia* (Expectations of private ownership transformation, and their confrontation to reality), (Warsaw: Centrum Badania Opinii Spolecznej).

Chadha, B., Coricelli, F., and Krajnyak, K., 1993, Economic restructuring, unemployment, and growth in a transition economy, *IMF Staff Papers* 40(4): 744–80.

Cohen, D., and Saint-Paul, G., 1995, Uneven technical progress and job destruction, mimeo, Delta, Paris.

Commander, S., and Coricelli, F., 1995, *Unemployment, Restructuring, and the Labor Market in Eastern Europe and Russia* (Washington, DC: EDI, World Bank).

Commander, S., and Dhar, S., 1996, Enterprises in the Polish transition, mimeo, World Bank.

Commander, S., and McHale, J., 1996, Expropriating managers, worker influence and employment bias in a transitional firm, mimeo, World Bank.

Commander, S., and Tolstopiatenko, A., 1996, Restructuring and taxation in transition economies, mimeo, World Bank.

Commander, S., Dhar, S., and Yemtsov, R., 1996, How Russian firms make their wage and employment decisions, in Simon Commander, Qimiao Fan, and Mark Schaffer (eds.), *Enterprise Restructuring and Economic Policy in Russia* (Washington, DC: EDI, World Bank).

Coricelli, F., 1995, Fiscal issues in economies in transition: the case of Central-Eastern Europe, mimeo, CEPR, London.

Davis, S., Haltiwanger, J., and Schuh, S., 1996, *Job Creation and Job Destruction* (Cambridge, MA: MIT Press).

De Melo, M., Denizer, C., and Gelb, A., 1995, From plan to market: patterns of transition, mimeo, World Bank.

Dewatripont, M., and Roland, G., 1992, Economic reform and dynamic political constraints, *Review of Economic Studies* 59: 703–30.

Earle, J., and Rose, R., 1996, Ownership transformation, economic behavior, and political attitudes in Russia, mimeo.

Estrin, S., and Svejnar, J., 1996, Employment and wage determination in the early years of transition: a comparative study, mimeo, World Bank.

EBRD, 1994, *Annual Transition Report 1994* (European Bank for Reconstruction and Development).

—— 1995, *Annual Transition Report 1995* (European Bank for Reconstruction and Development).

Fidrmuc, J., 1996, Political sustainability of economic reforms: dynamics and analysis of regional economic factors, Discussion Paper 9674, Tillburg University.

Fischer, S., Sahay, R., and Végh, C. A., 1996, Stabilization and growth in transition economies: the early experience, *Journal of Economic Perspectives* 10(2): 45–66.

Flemming, J., 1993, Relative price shocks and unemployment: arguments for temporarily reduced payroll taxes or protection, mimeo, EBRD.

Freeman, R., and Katz, L., 1991, Industrial wage and employment determination in an open economy, pp. 235–59 in J. Abowd and R. Freeman (eds.), *Immigration, Trade and the Labor Market* (Chicago, IL: NBER and University of Chicago Press).

Frydman, R., Pistor, K., and Rapaczynski, A., 1995, Investing in insider-dominated firms: a study of voucher privatization funds in Russia, in R. Frydman *et al.* (eds.), *Corporate Governance in*

Central Europe and Russia (Oxford: Central European University Press and Oxford University Press).

Gomulka, S., 1994, The financial situation of Polish enterprises and its impact on monetary and fiscal policies 1992–1993, *Economics of Transition* 2(2): 189–208.

Greif, A., and Kandel, E., 1994, Contract enforcement institutions: historical perspective and current status in Russia, ch. 8 in E. Lazear (ed.), *Economic Transition in Eastern Europe and Russia: Realities of Reform* (Stanford, CA: Hoover Institution Press).

Grosfeld, I., and Roland, G., 1994, Defensive and strategic restructuring in Central European enterprises, mimeo, Delta, Paris.

Grossman, S., and Hart, O., 1980, Takeover bids, the free rider problem and the theory of the corporation, *Bell Journal of Economics* 11: 42–64.

Halpern, L., and Wyplosz, C., 1994, Exchange rate policies in transition economies: in search of equilibrium, mimeo, IMF.

Harris, J., and Todaro, M., 1970, Migration, unemployment and development: a two-sector analysis, *American Economic Review* 60(1).

IMF, 1994, *World Economic Outlook* (October) (Washington, DC: IMF).

—— 1996, *World Economic Outlook* (May) (Washington, DC: IMF).

Jilek, J., 1995, The quality and availability of official statistical data, pp. 103–19 in Jan Svejnar (ed.), *The Czech Republic and Economic Transition in Eastern Europe* (Academic Press).

Johnson, S., and Loveman, G., 1995, *Starting over in Eastern Europe: Entrepreneurship and Economic Renewal* (Cambridge, MA: Harvard Business School Press).

Katz, B., and Owen, J., 1993, Privatization: choosing the optimal path, *Journal of Comparative Economics* 17: 715–36.

Kaufmann, D., and Kaliberda, A., 1995, Integrating the unofficial economy into the dynamics of post-socialist economies: a framework of analysis and evidence, mimeo, World Bank.

Keeling, J., 1996, Fiscal policy in transition, MA thesis, MIT.

Köllô, J., 1995a, Firing, hiring and wage growth in Hungarian firms, mimeo, Institute of Economics, Hungarian Academy of Sciences, Budapest.

Köllô, J., 1995b, Short-term response of employment to sales in state-owned and private firms in Hungary 1990–1994, mimeo, Institute of Economics, Hungarian Academy of Sciences, Budapest.

—— 1996, Employment, wage setting in three stages of Hungary's labour market transition, mimeo, Institute of Economics, Hungarian Academy of Sciences, Budapest.

Konings, J., Lehman, H., and Schaffer, M., 1995, Employment growth, job creation and job destruction in Polish industry: 1988–91, mimeo.

Kornai, J., 1994, Transformational recession: a general phenomenon examined through the example of Hungary's development, Discussion Paper 1, Collegium Budapest.

Laski, K., 1993, Fiscal policy and effective demand during transformation, Working Paper 189, WIW, Vienna.

Layard, R., and Richter, A., 1995, How much unemployment is needed for restructuring: the Russian experience, *Economics of Transition* 3(1) (March): 39–58.

Lilien, D., 1982, Sectoral shifts and cyclical unemployment, *Journal of Political Economy* 90: 777–92.

Lizal, L., Singer, M., and Svejnar, J., 1995, Manager interests, breakups and performance of state enterprises in transition, pp. 211–32 in Jan Svejnar (ed.), *The Czech Republic and Economic Transition in Eastern Europe* (Academic Press).

Maret, X., and Schwartz, G., 1994, Poland: social protection and the pension system during the transition, *International Social Security Review* 2: 51–69.

Murphy, K., Shleifer, A., and Vishny, R., 1992, The transition to a market economy: pitfalls of partial reform, *Quarterly Journal of Economics* 107(3): 889–906.

Mussa, M., 1986, The adjustment process and the timing of trade liberalization, pp. 68–124 in A. Choski and D. Papageorgiou (eds.), *Economic Reform in Developing Countries* (Oxford: Basil Blackwell).

Neary, J., 1982, Intersectoral capital mobility, wage stickiness and the case for adjustment assistance in J. Bhagwati (ed.), *Import Competition and Response* (Chicago, IL: University of Chicago Press).

Nuti, D., 1996, Inflation, interest and exchange rates in transition, *Economics of Transition* 4(1): 137–58.

OECD, 1992, *Economic Survey: Poland 1992* (Paris: OECD).

——1996, *Short Term Indicators* 2 (Paris: OECD).

Pohl, G., Djankov, S., and Anderson, R., 1996, Restructuring large industrial firms in Central and Eastern Europe: an empirical analysis, World Bank Technical Paper 332.

Rodrik, D., 1994, Foreign trade in Eastern Europe's transition: early results, pp. 319–56 in O. Blanchard, K. Froot, and J. Sachs (eds.), *The Transition in Eastern Europe*, vol. 2 (Chicago, IL: NBER and University of Chicago Press).

Roland, G., 1996, Economic efficiency and political constraints in privatization and restructuring, mimeo, ECARE and CEME, Brussels.

Ruggerone, L., 1996, Unemployment and inflationary finance dynamics at the early stages of transition, *Economic Journal* 106: 438–94.

Sachs, J., 1993, *Poland's Jump to the Market Economy* (Cambridge, MA: MIT Press).

Sachs, J., and Warner, A., 1996, Achieving rapid growth in the transition economies of Central Europe, Discussion Paper 544, HIID, Cambridge, MA.

Schaffer, M., 1992, The enterprise sector and emergence of the Polish fiscal crisis 1990–91, mimeo, CEP, LSE.

Senik-Leygonie, C., and Duflo, E., 1996, Industrial restructuring in Russia: early reactions of firms to the shock of liberalization, mimeo, MIT and Delta.

Shapiro, C., and Stiglitz, J., 1984, Equilibrium unemployment as a discipline device, *American Economic Review* 74: 433–44.

Shimer, R., 1995, Microfoundations of the optimal speed of transition, mimeo, MIT.

Shleifer, A., 1997, Government in transition, *European Economic Review*, Schumpeter lecture, forthcoming.

Shleifer, A., and Vishny, R., 1986, Large shareholders and corporate control, *Journal of Political Economy* 94(3-1): 461–88.

——1993, Corruption, *Quarterly Journal of Economics* 108(3): 599–618.

Index